Wise sayings from
JEWISH WISDOM:

If you love the things you do, you don't age, you always remain young. Age is for the calendar.

—SOL HUROK

God created Paradise and said, "The boastful may not enter."

—MOSES IBN EZRA

Each child carries his own blessing into the world.

—*Yiddish saying*

God does not play dice with the world.

—ALBERT EINSTEIN

By David C. Gross:

PRIDE OF OUR PEOPLE: A New Selection of 36 Life
    Stories of Outstanding, Contemporary Jewish
    Men and Jewish Women

LAUGHING THROUGH THE YEARS: A New
    Treasury of Jewish Humor

JEWISH WISDOM: A Treasury of Proverbs, Maxims,
    Aphorisms, Wise Sayings, and Memorable
    Quotations

JEWISH WISDOM

A TREASURY OF PROVERBS, MAXIMS, APHORISMS, WISE SAYINGS, AND MEMORABLE QUOTATIONS

Compiled by David C. Gross
and Esther R. Gross

FAWCETT CREST • NEW YORK

A Fawcett Crest Book
Published by Ballantine Books
Copyright © 1992 by David C. Gross

http://www.randomhouse.com

Library of Congress Catalog Card Number: 91-46069

ISBN 0-449-22206-3

This edition published by arrangement with Walker and Company

Printed in Canada

Cover art courtesy of the Jewish Museum/Art Resource, New York

First Ballantine Books Edition: December 1993

10 9 8 7 6

For all people who agree
with the Talmudic dictum:
"The highest wisdom is
kindness."

PREFACE

King Solomon wrote that his Book of Proverbs (in the Hebrew Bible), which has been studied for many centuries by scores of millions of people, in many hundreds of translations from the original Hebrew, was intended for "learning wisdom and discipline," and for "acquiring success, righteousness, justice, and equity," and also for "endowing the simple with shrewdness, the young with knowledge and foresight."

Assembled in this book are more than one thousand proverbs, wise sayings, and memorable quotations, from the past and from our own time, all meant to advance wisdom and understanding. These entries may instruct, inspire, guide, and even lead the reader to the good life; at the very least, they will open up a whole new dimension of self-exploration.

There is a centuries-old Jewish tradition that says that God does not destroy the cruel world in which we live for the sake of the thirty-six anonymous, righteous people who exist in every generation. The identity of these thirty-six is unknown, often even to themselves, and yet, somehow, they serve as role models for all people striving for a better life. In other words, this book is not for the thirty-six—usually called the *Lamed Vavniks*—but for all the rest of us.

In nearly four thousand years of turbulent history, the Jewish people have learned a thing or two, lessons that can come under the heading of "Jewish wisdom." These are encapsulated in proverbs, words of advice, and memorable quotations. By and large, these words of guidance are designed to lead to a happy, serene, fulfilling life, not only for Jews but for all people.

These proverbs and wise sayings seek to help us improve our character, deepen our understanding of life, and expand our wisdom so that we will become better people, enjoy life more, and make this world a happier, more just place. We are advised to be hopeful, cheerful, and at the same time, realistic. One of the lines in the

Book of Proverbs says: "Even in laughter, the heart aches."

Each reader of this book will respond individually to the various entries, which encompass a wide variety of subjects. Some of the entries will probably be seen as bittersweet, some as droll, some may even appear naive; to some people some may even border on the cynical. Be assured, however, that all the entries are the result of long years of individual and collective experience, and they are offered with the very best of intentions.

Jewish Wisdom is for any person, Jew or Gentile, seeking to expand his or her wisdom. We trust that this volume will bring in its wake serenity, hope, and joy.

It was Ecclesiastes who wrote a very long time ago: "The sayings of the wise are like goads, like nails fixed in prodding sticks. They were given by one Shepherd."

D. C. G. and E. R. G.

ABILITY

Even an angel cannot do two things at the same time.
—*Genesis Rabbah*

ABSTINENCE

Do not abstain from your time of prosperity, and do not let the good fortune escape you.
—*Wisdom of Sirach*

Whoever denies himself a little wine is a sinner—and the man who denies himself too many things is a greater sinner.

—*Talmud*

ACCUSATION

An accuser may not act as a defender.

—*Talmud*

God detests a man who rushes to accuse a neighbor.

—*Talmud*

ACTION

Action is what matters. We are present where we act.

—*Henri Bergson*

God is present in every action and in every thought.

—*Rabbi Nahman of Bratslav*

Through faith man experiences the meaning of the world; through action he is to give it meaning.

—*Leo Baeck*

Act while you can—while you have the chance, the means, and the strength.

—*Simeon ben Eliezar*

ADVERSITY

There is no education like adversity.

—*Benjamin Disraeli*

ADVICE

Beware of unsolicited advice.

—*Rabbi Akiva*

Teach your tongue to say "I don't know," rather than invent something.

—*Talmud*

AGE

I will never be an old man. To me, old age is always fifteen years older than I am.

—*Bernard Baruch*

If you love the things you do, you don't age, you always remain young. Age is for the calendar.

—*Sol Hurok*

The hoary head is a crown of glory.

—*Proverbs*

Old age is like a plane flying through a storm. Once you're aboard, there's nothing you can do.

—*Golda Meir*

At five years of age, study Scripture; at ten, study Mishna; at thirteen, fulfill the commandments; at fifteen, study Talmud; at eighteen, get married; at twenty, seek a livelihood; at thirty, enter into your full strength; at forty, reach understanding; at fifty, prepare to give counsel; at sixty, you attain old age; at seventy, your hair turns white; at eighty, you acquire the gift of

special strength; at ninety, you bend under the weight of years; at one hundred, it is as if you are already dead and have departed from this world.
—*Ethics of the Fathers*

ALTRUISM

Only a life lived for others is a life worthwhile.
—*Albert Einstein*

My fathers planted for me, and I planted for my children.
—*Talmud*

AMBITION

Look for cake, and lose your bread.
—*Yiddish saying*

Ambition destroys its possessor.
—*Talmud*

Man strives, and God laughs.
—*Yiddish saying*

Man's ambition to add to his wealth and honor is the chief source of his misery.

—*Maimonides*

ANCESTRY

I am a Jew. When the ancestors of the right honorable gentleman [Daniel O'Connell, a parliamentary opponent] were living as savages in an unknown island, mine were priests in the Temple of Solomon.

—*Benjamin Disraeli*

God prefers your deeds to your ancestors' virtues.

—*Genesis Rabbah*

ANGER

God Himself prays, "May my mercy overcome my anger."

—*Abba Aricha*

Anger deprives a sage of his wisdom, a prophet of his vision.

—*Simeon ben Lakish*

Anger kills the foolish man.

—*Job*

Anger in a house is like a worm in a plant.

—*Talmud*

ANIMALS

A good man will not sell an animal to a cruel man.

—*Judah ben Samuel*

Do not eat before you have fed your animal.

—*Talmud*

ANXIETY

The cure for anxiety about the future is not nostalgia for the past.

—*Mordecai Kaplan*

Riches bring anxiety; wisdom brings peace of mind.

—*Solomon ibn Gabirol*

APATHY

You shall not stand idly by the blood of your neighbor.

—*Leviticus*

When you are apathetic to crimes committed against others, you have dug a pit for yourself.

—*Sholem Asch*

APPEARANCE

Man looks at the external appearance, but God looks at the heart.

—*Samuel I*

Do not laud a man for his good looks, and do not hate a man for his appearance.

—*Wisdom of Sirach*

A homely patch is nicer than a beautiful hole.
— *Yiddish saying*

ARROGANCE

How great some men would be if they were not arrogant.

— *Talmud*

ART

Religion is the everlasting dialogue between God and man. Art is its soliloquy.

— *Franz Werfel*

The artist must penetrate into the world, feel the fate of human beings, of people, with real love. There is no art for art's sake—one must be interested in the whole realm of life.

— *Marc Chagall*

ATHEISM

The fool has said in his heart, "There is no God."

—*Psalms*

The soul of man does not thrive on godlessness.

—*Harry Wolfson*

AUTHORITY

The ancient authorities are entitled to a vote, but not to a veto.

—*Mordecai Kaplan*

The great majority of people have a strong need for authority which they can admire, to which they can submit, and which even sometimes mistreats them. It is the longing for the father that lives in each of us from childhood days.

—*Sigmund Freud*

It is not by a perpetual Amen to every utterance of a great authority that truth or literature gains anything.

—*Solomon Schechter*

BACHELOR

Man is not even called man until he is united with a woman.

—*Zohar*

It is not good for a man to be alone.

—*Genesis*

BEAUTY

Beauty is a fading flower.

—*Isaiah*

Grace is deceitful, and beauty is vain.

—*Proverbs*

The mind needs to relax by contemplating pictures and other beautiful objects.

—*Maimonides*

A beautiful ornament looks best on a beautiful woman.

—*Talmud*

Beauty is the outward form of truth.
—*Grace Aquilar*

BEGINNING

All beginnings are hard.
—*Mekilta (Exodus)*

A daring beginning is halfway to winning.
—*Heinrich Heine*

BEHAVIOR

There is no truer index to intelligence than good behavior.

—*Solomon ibn Gabirol*

Circumstances are beyond the control of man but his conduct is in his own power.
—*Benjamin Disraeli*

BELIEF

Belief cannot be commanded.
—*Samuel Luzzatto*

Faith is not commanded. Where the question is of eternal truth, there is nothing said of believing but *understanding* and *knowing*.
—*Moses Mendelssohn*

BIBLE

The Bible is the Magna Carta of humanity.
—*Henry George*

The Bible is an extraordinary book, expressing many norms and principles that have maintained their validity throughout thousands of years. It proclaimed a vision of faith for men that is still valid and awaiting realization.
—*Erich Fromm*

We have preserved the Book, and the Book has preserved us.

—*David Ben Gurion*

BIRTH

Man enters and departs this life crying and weeping. He comes and he leaves in love and ignorance.

—*Ecclesiastes*

The world is new to us every morning—this is God's gift, and every person should believe he is reborn every day.

—*Baal Shem Tov*

BLESSING

All blessings begin, "Blessed be Thou," as though the person were speaking to a close friend.

—*Eleazar ben Judah of Worms*

The Lord bless you and keep you. The Lord make His face to shine upon you and be gra-

cious unto you. The Lord lift up His counte-
nance upon you and give you peace.

—Numbers

BLISS

If a person knew at twenty how fortunate he
is to be twenty, he would get a stroke because
of sheer bliss.

—Arthur Schnitzler

BLOOD

He who sheds blood impairs the divine image.

—Rabbi Akiva

Woe to him that builds a town with blood.

—Habakuk

BOASTING

God created Paradise and said, "The boastful
may not enter."

—Moses ibn Ezra

Wisdom departs from a boastful sage, and prophecy from a boastful prophet.

—*Talmud*

He who advertises his name, loses it.

—*Ethics of the Fathers*

BODY

If you marvel at the waters of the sea, that the sweet and the salty do not mingle, think of the tiny head, where the fluids of its many fountains do not mingle.

—*Numbers Rabbah*

What a marvelous machine it is, the human body. A chemical laboratory, a power house. Every movement, voluntary or involuntary, full of secrets and marvels!

—*Theodor Herzl*

BOLDNESS

(Asked what book he would choose if he were shipwrecked on a desert island): A practical guide to boat building.

—*Bernard Baruch*

BOOKS

A book may be as great a thing as a battle.
—*Benjamin Disraeli*

My pen is my harp and my lyre; my library is my garden and my orchard.

—*Judah Halevi*

BORROWING

The borrower is a servant to the lender.
—*Proverbs*

Lend money and acquire an enemy.
—*Yiddish saying*

A borrower may not lend the thing he borrowed.

—Talmud

BREAD

Man does not live by bread alone.

—Deuteronomy

Cast your bread upon the waters, for you shall find it after many days.

—Ecclesiastes

BRIBE

If you grease the wheels, you can ride.

—Shalom Aleichem

While accepting bribes to do injustice is an act of utter depravity, to accept them to do justice shows half-depravity.

—Philo

BROTHERHOOD

The highest ideal of Judaism is the universal brotherhood of man.

—*Samson Raphael Hirsch*

Have we not all one Father? Has not one God created us all?

—*Malachi*

How good and how pleasant it is for brethren to live together in unity.

—*Psalms*

Better a neighbor who is near than a brother who is far off.

—*Proverbs*

All Jews, including proselytes, are like brothers.

—*Maimonides*

BURDEN

Man himself assumes the burden under which he falls.

—*Abraham ibn Ezra*

Cast your burden upon the Lord, and He will sustain you.

—*Psalms*

CANDOR

There is no wisdom like frankness.

—*Benjamin Disraeli*

CAPITAL PUNISHMENT

Choose an easy death for one who must be executed.

—*Talmud*

Whoever sheds man's blood, by man shall his blood be shed.

—*Genesis*

CAUTION

Caution should not be overcautious.
—*Bahya ibn Pakuda*

He who observes the wind shall sow, and he who regards the clouds shall not reap.
—*Ecclesiastes*

Be not like the bird that sees the seed, but not the trap.

—*Judah ibn Tibbon*

CEMETERY

Cemeteries must not be treated disrespectfully. Cattle may not feed there, nor a watercourse turned, nor grass plucked.
—*Talmud*

It is forbidden to use the cemetery for any other purpose, (such as) to eat, drink, work, read Torah, or study Mishna there.

—*Maimonides*

CEREMONY

A ceremony is not adequately discharged unless it is performed with beauty and dignity.

—*Moses Luzzatto*

Ceremonies are no aid to blessedness.

—*Baruch Spinoza*

Our ceremonialism is a training in self-conquest, while it links the generations and unifies (the Jews), dispersed to the four corners of the earth, as nothing else could.

—*Israel Zangwill*

CHANCE

Time and chance happen to all.

—*Ecclesiastes*

If you win, you win a charcoal; if you lose, you lose a pearl.

—*Talmud*

CHANGE

A change of name or place may sometimes save a person.

—*Talmud*

Like language, a religion was dead when it ceased to change.

—*Israel Zangwill*

CHAOS

Our soul is a vast panorama. There is room for so much in us at the same time: Love and treachery, faith and faithlessness, adoration of one person and longing for another, or for several others. We try to bring order into ourselves as best we can, but this order is, after all, something artificial. Our natural state is chaos.

—*Arthur Schnitzler*

CHARACTER

Three kinds my soul hates: A poor man who is proud, a rich man who lies, an old man who is an adulterer.

—*Wisdom of Sirach*

Every man must strive first for the improvement of his own character, and then of the character of others.

—*Moses ibn Ezra*

Character is shaped by deeds, and character is partly habit.

—*Claude Montefiore*

God decides what shall befall a person, but not whether he will be righteous or evil.

—*Talmud*

CHARITY

You shall not harden your heart nor shut your hand from your needy brother, but lend him sufficient for his need.

—*Deuteronomy*

Care of the poor is incumbent on society.

—*Baruch Spinoza*

He who gives to the poor shall not be lacking.

—*Proverbs*

Even a poor man, a recipient of charity, should give charity.

—*Talmud*

The more charity, the more peace.

—*Hillel*

The greatest charity is to enable the poor to earn a living.

—*Talmud*

I always give much away and so gather happiness instead of pleasure.

—*Rachel Varnhagen*

CHARM

Three possess charm: A place to its residents, a woman to her husband, a bargain to a customer.

—*Talmud*

Charm is more than beauty.

—*Yiddish saying*

Charm is character exercising its influence.

—*Edgar Magnin*

CHILDREN

Let not the fear of bad offspring deter you. You do your duty, and the Holy One will do what pleases Him.

—*Talmud*

Each child carries his own blessing into the world.

—Yiddish saying

Childhood and youth are vanity.

—Ecclesiastes

Train a child in the way he should go, and when he is old he will not depart from it.

—Proverbs

What a child says on the street, the parents say at home.

—Talmud

CHOICE

Everything is foreseen, yet freedom of choice is granted. The world is judged favorably, yet all depends on the preponderance of good deeds.

—Rabbi Akiva

CLEANLINESS

Who shall ascend the mountain of the Lord?
He who has clean hands and a pure heart.

—*Psalms*

A soldier must admire the singular attention
that was paid to the rules of cleanliness (in ancient Israel).

—*George Washington*

Dirty hands are unfit for reciting grace.

—*Talmud*

CLEVERNESS

When wisdom enters, subtlety comes along.

—*Talmud*

To want to be the cleverest of all is the biggest
folly.

—*Shalom Aleichem*

CLOTHING

In your community, your reputation matters. In a strange place, your clothing counts.

—*Talmud*

The clothes of a wise man must be free of blemishes. He should not don the clothing of princes to attract attention, nor should he dress like a pauper, which would lead to disrespect.

—*Maimonides*

COMMANDMENTS

The important thing is not how many separate commandments we obey, but the spirit in which we obey them.

—*Baal Shem Tov*

All the 613 commandments are included in the Ten Commandments.

—*Rashi*

Be as strict in observing a light command-ment as a major one, for you do not know their relative reward.

—*Judah Hanassi*

The commandments are interwoven and sup-plement each other; they are one command-ment, one single truth.

—*Vilna Gaon*

COMMERCE

When prices drop, buy.

—*Talmud*

Merchants throughout the world have the same religion.

—*Heinrich Heine*

The old idea of a good bargain was a trans-action in which one man got the better of an-other. The new idea of a good contract is a transaction which is good for both parties.

—*Louis D. Brandeis*

This is the manner of merchants: first they show the poor stuff, and then they show the best.

—Rashi

COMMON SENSE

Common sense is the root of wisdom.
—Samuel Hanagid

Man's best gift is his common sense.
—Moses ibn Ezra

Lost common sense cannot be regained.
—Solomon ibn Gabirol

COMMUNITY

The yearning of Judaism for God is the yearning to prepare a resting place for Him in genuine community. Judaism's understanding of Israel is that genuine community will spring from that people. Its messianic expectation is the expectation of genuine community, fully realized.

—Martin Buber

Do not withdraw from the community.

—*Hillel*

Join a community—only in this way can your work be made universal and eternal.

—*Samson Raphael Hirsch*

The community is Israel's rampart.

—*Talmud*

The wolf will grasp the sheep that leaves the flock.

—*Moses ibn Ezra*

COMPANION

Give me friendship or give me death.

—*Talmud*

When one of my friends perished, one of my limbs died.

—*Solomon ibn Gabirol*

COMPASSION

Where there is no compassion, crime increases.

—*Rabbi Nahman of Bratslav*

A person who seeks help for a friend, while needy himself, will be answered first.

—*Talmud*

COMPENSATION

Exact no fee for teaching Torah. God gave it gratis.

—*Talmud*

COMPROMISE

The gains of compromise are nothing compared to its losses.

—*Chofetz Chaim*

CONCEIT

Woe unto them that are wise in their own eyes.

—*Isaiah*

Pride goes before destruction, and a haughty spirit before a fall.

—*Proverbs*

Haughtiness toward men is rebellion to God.

—*Nahmanides*

CONDUCT

The way a man walks reveals whether he is wise or foolish, learned or ignorant.

—Maimonides

CONFESSION

To confess one's sins is to honor the Holy One.

—Talmud

If anything discreditable be in you, be the first to tell it

—Talmud

CONFIDENCE

Don't be too sure of yourself until the day you die.

—*Hillel*

CONSCIENCE

A good digestion depends on a good conscience.

—*Benjamin Disraeli*

Real human progress depends not so much on inventive ingenuity, as on conscience.

—*Albert Einstein*

One pang of conscience is worth more than many lashes.

—*Talmud*

Be the master of your will, and the slave of your conscience.

—*Hassidic saying*

CONSISTENCY

Whatever the faults of the rabbis, consistency was not one of them.

—*Solomon Schechter*

CONTENTMENT

Who is rich? He who rejoices in his lot.

—*Ethics of the Fathers*

Be contented with much or with little, and you will not hear the reproach of being a stranger—it is a miserable life to go from house to house. Where you are a stranger, you cannot open your mouth.

—*Wisdom of Sirach*

Three things soften a person's heart: A pleasing melody, a pleasant scene, and a fragrant odor.

—*Talmud*

CONTROVERSY

He who is unyielding in a dispute is a sinner.

—*Talmud*

A struggle that revolves around the Bible ends in love.

—*Rashi*

A nation without controversy is politically dead.

—*Herbert Samuel*

COURAGE

No sickness of the soul is worse than discouragement. Man must continually renew the idea of courage in his mind.

—*Israel Salanter*

Those who train themselves in wisdom cultivate true courage.

—*Philo*

COURTESY

It is not an act of courtesy to carry the cane for the cripple.

—*Arthur Schnitzler*

CRITICISM

Do not rebuke a scorner, lest he despise you. Rebuke a wise man, and he will love you.

—*Proverbs*

A man can see a speck on someone's hair, but cannot see the flies on his own nose.

—*Mendele Mocher Seforim*

CRUELTY

It is cruel not to forgive a person who begs for forgiveness.

—*Rashi*

CURSE

Let yourself be cursed, rather than curse.

—*Talmud*

As the wandering sparrow, as the flying swallow, so the curse that is baseless shall not come home.

—*Proverbs*

CUSTOM

Neither Scripture nor primitive Judaism, but general custom forms the real rule of Jewish practice.

—*Solomon Schechter*

See how the people act, and that is the law.
—*Talmud*

Customs are stronger than laws.
—*Talmud*

CYNICISM

The so-called sophisticate who prides himself on cynicism is only seeking to escape his own inadequacies.
—*Edgar Magnin*

Cynicism is idealism gone sour.
—*Will Herberg*

If you want people to like you, agree with them.
—*Hassidic saying*

DANGER

Three need to be guarded: A patient, a groom, and a bride.

—*Talmud*

It is wrong to consider personal danger when the public welfare is at stake.

—*Maimonides*

Breed not a savage dog, nor permit a loose stairway.

—*Talmud*

When the lion sleeps, don't wake him.

—*Yiddish saying*

DARKNESS

The only way of converting darkness into light is by giving to the poor.

—*Shneur Zalman*

The way of the wicked is all darkness; they do not know what will make them stumble.

—*Proverbs*

DAUGHTER

A mother is always attached to her daughter, but not so a daughter to her mother.

—*Talmud*

You reproach your daughter, but you mean your daughter-in-law.

—*Yiddish saying*

A daughter is to her father a treasure of sleeplessness.

—*Wisdom of Sirach*

It's easier to guard a sack of fleas than a maiden in love

—*Yiddish saying*

DEATH

Death is the means of transition to future life, which is the ultimate goal of mortal existence.
—*Saadiah Gaon*

A person should always see himself as if he is about to die, lest he die during a moment when he is a sinner and removed from God. Therefore he must return from his sin immediately.
—*Maimonides*

Death does not knock on the door.
—*Yiddish saying*

In the messianic future, there will be no death.
—*Genesis Rabbah*

DEBT

Scratching and borrowing money help, but only for a short time.
—*Yiddish saying*

Go to sleep without dinner, and wake up without debt.
—*Judah ibn Tibbon*

DECEIT

Rather a man die than lie.
—*Rabbi Nahman of Bratslav*

A liar's punishment is that he is not believed even when he is telling the truth.
—*Simeon bar Yochai*

It is forbidden to deceive anyone, Jew or Gentile.
—*Talmud*

Verbal fraud is worse than monetary fraud.
—*Talmud*

DEEDS

Jewish piety and Jewish wisdom are found only where the soul is in the possession of the unity of devotion and deed.

—*Leo Baeck*

Say little and do much.

—*Shammai*

The divine sings in noble deeds.
> —*Abraham Joshua Heschel*

Everything depends on deeds.
> —*Rabbi Akiva*

Deeds—not talk—count.
> —*Ethics of the Fathers*

DEFENSE

If someone comes to kill you, rise up early and kill him first.
> —*Talmud*

DESCENDANTS

Every American Jew who aids in advancing the Jewish settlement in Palestine, though he feels that neither he nor his descendants will ever live there, will be a better man and a better American for doing so.
> —*Louis D. Brandeis*

Fruits take after their roots.

—*Abraham ibn Ezra*

DESIRE

Desires must be purified and idealized, not eradicated.

—*Vilna Gaon*

Desire blinds the wise.

—*Abraham ibn Ezra*

Worldly desires are like columns of sunshine radiating through a dusty window, nothing tangible, nothing more.

—*Rabbi Nahman of Bratslav*

DESTINY

If a man is destined to drown, he will drown even in a spoonful of water.

—*Yiddish saying*

I believe that if it would rain money from heaven, the coins would knock holes in my head.

—*Heinrich Heine*

To be a Jew is a destiny.

—*Vicki Baum*

DICTATORSHIP

Torah can be interpreted in 49 varied ways. God told Moses, "Decide according to the majority."

—*Talmud*

We must not appoint a leader over the community without first consulting the people.

—*Talmud*

DIFFICULTIES

He who wishes to be a real Jew must go to the Land of Israel—despite all the difficulties and obstacles.

—*Rabbi Nahman of Bratslav*

DIGNITY

Love forgets dignity.

—*Talmud*

To be invested with dignity means to represent something more than oneself.

—*Abraham Joshua Heschel*

DISCRETION

A jewel in a pig's nose is comparable to a pretty woman without discretion.

—*Proverbs*

When you speak at night, lower your voice. When you speak by day, look around first.

—*Solomon ibn Gabirol*

DISEASE

Life is a terrible disease, curable only by death.

—*Hai Gaon*

It is a serious disease to worry over what has not occurred.

—*Solomon ibn Gabirol*

The words of Torah heal the soul, not the body.

—*Maimonides*

DISPUTE

Do not respond to a barking dog.

—*Moroccan Jewish saying*

One hundred people can sit together peacefully, but two dogs in the same place will pick a fight.

—*Kurdistan Jewish saying*

DIVORCE

No man may divorce his wife unless he found her guilty of an immoral act.

—*Shammai*

A man may divorce his wife if he finds another woman more beautiful.

—*Rabbi Akiva*

He who sends away his wife is hateful.

—*Talmud*

A man may divorce his wife merely for spoiling his food.

—*Hillel*

If a woman says, "My husband is distasteful to me, I cannot live with him," the court compels the husband to divorce her, because a wife is not a captive.

—*Maimonides*

When a divorced man marries a divorced woman, there are four people in that marital bed.

—*Talmud*

DUTY

Whoever performs only his duty is not doing his duty.

—*Bahya ibn Pakuda*

It is not required that you complete a task, but neither are you exempt from beginning it.

—*Ethics of the Fathers*

DRUNKENNESS

A worker prone to drinking will never grow rich.

—*Wisdom of Sirach*

Wine mocks, strong drink brawls. No one under the influence is wise.

—*Proverbs*

EATING

Man eats to live, he does not live to eat.
—*Abraham ibn Ezra*

Don't dance before you eat.
—*Shalom Aleichem*

Food is better than drink up to the age of forty. After forty, drink is better.
—*Talmud*

EDUCATION

In time, even a bear can be taught to dance.
—*Yiddish saying*

A village without a school should be abolished.
—*Talmud*

In an unlettered world, when even kings could not sign their names, Jews had already developed a system of universal education, so that an illiterate Jew—even in the Dark Ages—was a contradiction in terms.

—*Cecil Roth*

ENEMY

As a man prays for himself, so must he pray for his enemy.

—*Baal Shem Tov*

A needle's eye is not too small for two lovers, but the whole world is not big enough for two enemies.

—*Solomon ibn Gabirol*

If two men claim your help, and one is your enemy, help him first.

—*Talmud*

ENJOYMENT

Even one hour in the Garden of Eden is enjoyable.

—Yiddish saying

Man was not brought into this world to enjoy himself.

—Abraham ibn Ezra

In this world, life is known only once—not twice.

—Yiddish saying

ENVY

Do not envy a lawless man, or choose any of his ways, for the devious man is an abomination to the Lord.

—Proverbs

Envious wives will ruin their husbands.

—Leviticus Rabbah

The man who envies is guilty of robbery in thought.

—*Rabbi Nahman of Bratslav*

EQUALITY

Your servant should be your equal. You should not eat white bread and he black bread. You should not drink old wine and he new wine. You should not sleep on a feather bed, and he on straw.

—*Abbaye*

Equality is the result of human organization. We are not born equal.

—*Hannah Arendt*

ETERNITY

We Jews are eternal wanderers, deeply rooted in our body and blood. It is this rootedness in ourselves and in nothing but ourselves that vouchsafes our eternity.

—*Franz Rosenzweig*

There is something higher than modernity, and that is eternity.

—*Solomon Schechter*

ETHICS

For the benefit of the flowers, we water the thorns, too.

—*Egyptian Jewish saying*

There is nothing better than a good reputation.

—*German Jewish saying*

A person with a clear conscience can sleep even in the desert.

—*Yemenite Jewish saying*

EVIL

The evil of the eye grows from the evil of the heart.

—*Abraham ibn Ezra*

The greater the man, the greater his evil inclination.

—*Talmud*

Keep three things in mind and you will escape the results of evil: Know where you came from, where you are going, and before Whom you will have to give a full account.

—*Ethics of the Fathers*

The evil urge lures men in this world, and then testifies against them in the next world.

—*Talmud*

Woe to them that call evil good, and good evil.

—*Isaiah*

EXCESS

There should be moderation even in excess.
—*Benjamin Disraeli*

Do not be too righteous, and do not be too wise.
—*Ecclesiastes*

There are three people whose lives are unworthy—the overly compassionate, the hottempered, and the hypercritical.

—*Talmud*

EXPERIENCE

Experience is a good school, but the fees are high.

—*Heinrich Heine*

Whoever does not try, does not learn.
—*Iraqi Jewish saying*

Experience costs blood.

—*Yiddish saying*

Don't ask the doctor; ask the patient.
—*Yiddish saying*

There is no one better than an experienced person.
—*Central European Jewish saying*

FACE

He who closes his eyes is hatching a scheme; he who tightens his lips is planning mischief.
—*Proverbs*

A pretty face is half a dowry.
—*Shalom Aleichem*

FAITH

In the struggle with evil, only faith matters.
—*Baal Shem Tov*

I am a Jew because the faith of Israel demands of me no abdication of the mind.
—*Edmond Fleg*

Through faith, man experiences the meaning of the world; through action, he is to give it a meaning.

—Leo Baeck

A man should believe in God through faith, not because of miracles.

—Rabbi Nahman of Bratslav

FAME

Good men do not need monuments. Their deeds remain their shrines.

—Talmud

He who seeks fame loses his name. Knowledge that does not grow will decrease. He who does not study deserves to die.

—Hillel

If you wish to live long, don't become famous.

—Baal Shem Tov

Fame always brings loneliness.

—Vicki Baum

FAMILY

Honor your father-in-law and mother-in-law for now they are your parents.

—*Tobit*

Nobody may interfere between two people who sleep on the same pillow.

—*Yiddish saying*

A brother helped by a brother is like a fortified city.

—*Proverbs*

A father loves his children, but they love their children.

—*Talmud*

Be fruitful and multiply, and replenish the earth.

—*Genesis*

FATHER

My son, heed the discipline of your father, and do not forsake the instruction of your mother.

—*Proverbs*

The only time a son should disobey his father is if the father orders him to commit a sin.

—*Talmud*

He who raises a child is to be called father, not the man who only gave it birth.

—*Exodus Rabbah*

When a father laments that his son has taken to evil ways, what should he do? Love him more than ever.

—*Baal Shem Tov*

63

FEAR

Coming close to a king is like coming close to a lion. Others will be afraid of you, but your fear will also be great.

—*Hai Gaon*

Fear of God is the gateway of faith.

—*Zohar*

The whole world is like a very narrow bridge, and the main thing is not to be afraid.

—*Rabbi Nahman of Bratslav*

The fear of the Lord is the beginning of knowledge.

—*Proverbs*

FLATTERY

A deceitful tongue brings destruction to itself, and a flattering mouth works its own ruin.

—Proverbs

He who flatters with laughter wants to see you cry.

—Moroccan Jewish saying

Whoever needs milk, bows to the animal.

—Yiddish saying

FOLLY

Man does not commit a sin unless he is possessed by folly.

—Talmud

If you talk too much, you'll talk folly.

—Yiddish saying

FOOD

More people die from overeating than from undernourishment.

—*Talmud*

Fools love to eat sweets.

—*German Jewish saying*

Every sickness begins in the stomach.

—*Yemenite Jewish saying*

Though not itself food, salt adds flavor to dishes. The same is true of Kabbalah (Jewish mysticism)—though scarcely comprehensible—and tasteless—in itself, it adds flavor to the Torah.

—*Shneur Zalman*

FOOL

Teaching a fool is like gluing a broken pot.
>   —*Wisdom of Sirach*

The world is in the hands of fools.
>   —*Talmud*

When a fool holds his tongue, he is thought to be wise.
>   —*Proverbs*

Any plan formulated in a hurry is foolish.
>   —*Rashi*

A wise man knows and asks; a fool does not know and does not ask.
>   —*Persian Jewish saying*

FORGIVENESS

The most beautiful thing a man can do is forgive.
—*Eleazar ben Judah of Worms*

Whoever confesses his sin, God will forgive him.

—*Yemenite Jewish saying*

In Judaism there is no vicarious atonement.
—*Nahida Remy*

FREEDOM

The greatest menace to freedom is an inert people.

—*Louis D. Brandeis*

Since the Exodus, freedom has always spoken with a Hebrew accent.

—*Heinrich Heine*

The service of God spells freedom.

—*Judah Halevi*

Freedom is the world of joy.
                    —*Rabbi Nahman of Bratslav*

Proclaim liberty throughout the land, unto all the inhabitants thereof.
                    —*Leviticus*

FRIEND

In speaking to a friend, say "You and I," and not "I and you."
                    —*Judah ben Samuel*

There are three types of friends: Some are like food—indispensable; some are like medicine—good occasionally; and some are like poison—to be avoided always.
                    —*Samuel Hanagid*

A man without friends is like a left hand without a right.
                    —*Solomon ibn Gabirol*

To pull a friend out of the mud, don't hesitate to get dirty.

—*Baal Shem Tov*

The best mirror is a trusted, old friend.

—*Sephardic saying*

FUTURE

I never think of the future—it comes fast enough.

—*Albert Einstein*

Not every cloud brings rain.

—*Kurdistan Jewish saying*

Do not embitter life today with tomorrow's worry.

—*Persian Jewish saying*

Under no circumstances can a person ensure himself of anything.

—*Yiddish saying*

GAMBLING

A gambler always loses—money, dignity, and time. And if he wins, he weaves a spider's web around himself.

—*Maimonides*

Gamblers do not contribute to the public welfare.

—*Talmud*

GENTILE

For a Jew to cheat a Gentile is worse than cheating a Jew. In addition to breaking the moral law, it brings Jews into a position of contempt.

—*Talmud*

It is as wrong to steal from Esau as from Israel.

—*Nahmanides*

As the Gentiles carry on, so do the Jews follow suit.

—Yiddish saying

GLORY

Thus says the Lord: Let not the wise man glory in his wisdom, let not the rich man glory in his riches, but let him who glories glory in this: that he understands and knows Me, that I am the Lord who practices steadfast love, justice and righteousness in the earth.

—Jeremiah

Those who pursue glory, glory escapes them. Often glory falls on those who did not seek it.

—Talmud

GOD

Whatever God does is for the best.

—Rabbi Akiva

Israel's mission is to teach the nations of the world that God is the source of all blessing.

—Samson Raphael Hirsch

Within me is the Lord.

—*Moses ibn Ezra*

Have we not all one father? Did not one God create us?

—*Malachi*

Beloved is man for he was created in the image of God.

—*Rabbi Akiva*

O Lord, where shall I find Thee? Hidden and exalted is Thy place; and where shall I not find Thee? Full of Thy glory is infinite space.

—*Judah Halevi*

You cannot find the depth of man's heart, then how can you search out God?

—*Judith*

GOLD

Gold has made many people careless.
—*Wisdom of Sirach*

Gold's father is dirt, but it considers itself noble.

—*Yiddish saying*

GOODNESS

Follow the way of the good and keep to the paths of the just, for the upright will inherit the earth.

—*Proverbs*

Seek the good in everyone; reveal it, bring it forth.

—*Rabbi Nahman of Bratslav*

If someone throws stones at you, throw back bread.

—*Yiddish saying*

Good deeds are better than credos.
—*Ethics of the Fathers*

GOSSIP

Gossip is more horrible than a capital crime.
—*Talmud*

Gossip kills three people: the bearer, the person talked about, and the listener.
—*Numbers Rabbah*

Even if the whole slanderous tale is not believed, half of it is.
—*Genesis Rabbah*

You surround your vineyard with thorns—place doors and locks on your mouth.
—*Wisdom of Sirach*

GOVERNMENT

No government can be long secure without a formidable opposition.

—*Benjamin Disraeli*

Do not place your trust in princes.

—*Psalms*

Safety lies in the counsel of multitudes.

—*Proverbs*

Don't live in a city run by scholars.

—*Rabbi Akiva*

Pray for the welfare of the government, since but for the fear of it, men would swallow one another alive.

—*Ethics of the Fathers*

GREATNESS

Before a man attains greatness, he must descend to lowliness.

—*Rabbi Nahman of Bratslav*

Greatness flees from someone who chases it, and follows whoever flees it.

—*Talmud*

The man who cannot accept criticism cannot become great.

—*Rabbi Nahman of Bratslav*

GREED

Avarice, ambition, lust, and the like are species of madness.

—*Baruch Spinoza*

A handful does not satisfy a lion.

—*Talmud*

Those who increase their flesh only increase food for worms.

—*Ethics of the Fathers*

GRIEF

One who causes grief to another man, it is as though he caused grief to the whole world, for man is a microcosm.

—*Judah ben Samuel*

Grief is like a wheel that goes around and around the world.

—*Rashi*

If we could not forget, we would never be free from grief.

—*Bahya ibn Pakuda*

GROWTH

What does not grow, declines.

—*Hillel*

Don't be in a hurry like the almond—the first to blossom, the last to ripen. Be like the mulberry—the last to blossom, the first to ripen.

—*Ahikar*

GUILT

Silence may be equivalent to confession.

—*Talmud*

The guilty man who denies his guilt doubles it.

—*Talmud*

HABIT

An old cat will never learn to dance.

—*Moroccan Jewish saying*

Habit and character are closely interwoven, habit becoming like a second nature.

—*Maimonides*

A sin repeated seems to be permitted.

—*Talmud*

A mule driver does not smell the stink of his animals.

—*Yemenite Jewish saying*

HAPPINESS

I do not desire happiness if it is an island in a sea of misery.

—*Theodor Herzl*

Bright eyes gladden the heart, good news fattens the bones.

—*Proverbs*

One day's happiness makes a man forget his troubles, and one day of troubles makes him forget his past happiness.

—*Wisdom of Sirach*

Happiness is found in a happy heart.

—*Persian Jewish saying*

HATRED

Six things the Lord hates; seven are an abomination to Him: A haughty bearing, a lying tongue, hands that shed innocent blood, a mind that hatches evil plots, feet that run to do evil, a false witness testifying lies, and one who incites brothers to quarrel.

—Proverbs

The Holy Temple was destroyed because of baseless hatred.

—Talmud

People hate when they do not understand.
—Moses ibn Ezra

A person who hates people is hated by them.
—Solomon ibn Gabirol

A slap from your friend is better than your enemy's kiss.

—Dutch Jewish saying

Hatred upsets the social order.

—*Simeon bar Yochai*

HEALTH

There is no wealth like health.

—*Wisdom of Sirach*

Three things spoil a man's health: worry, travel, and sin.

—*Talmud*

A sick person is a prisoner.

—*Yemenite Jewish saying*

The goal of good health is to enable a person to acquire wisdom.

—*Maimonides*

A joyful heart makes for good health; despondency dries up the bones.

—*Proverbs*

HEART

Melody and song lead the heart of man to God.

—*Rabbi Nahman of Bratslav*

Those who don't know how to weep with their whole heart don't know how to laugh either.

—*Golda Meir*

Words that come from the heart enter the heart.

—*Moses ibn Ezra*

The tongue is the heart's pen.

—*Bahya ibn Pakuda*

HEAVEN

Each people has as much heaven over its head as it has land under its feet.

—*Chaim Nahman Bialik*

Thus said the Lord: Heaven is My throne, and the earth My footstool.
—*Isaiah*

Better an hour of happiness in heaven than a life of pleasure on earth.
—*Ethics of the Fathers*

HELP

If you do not help a person with trouble, it is as though you have brought trouble to him.
—*Rabbi Nahman of Bratslav*

I can chew for you, my child, but you must swallow by yourself.
—*Hungarian Jewish saying*

Whoever does not help himself cannot help others.
—*Yemenite Jewish saying*

HEREAFTER

The world is like an inn; the world to come, like home.

—*Talmud*

When a person leaves this world, he is accompanied not by silver, gold, or jewels, but by Torah and good deeds.

—*Ethics of the Fathers*

Plan for this world as if you plan to live forever. Plan for the hereafter as if you expect to die tomorrow.

—*Solomon ibn Gabirol*

HEROISM

No man is a hero to his relatives.

—*Israel Zangwill*

Who is a hero? He who masters his passions.

—*Ethics of the Fathers*

HISTORY

The God of history and the God of nature cannot be separated, and the Land of Israel is a token of their unity.

—*Martin Buber*

Read no history, only biography, for that is life without theory.

—*Benjamin Disraeli*

History has no time to be just. She keeps her eyes fixed on the victorious and leaves the vanquished in the shadows.

—*Stefan Zweig*

HOLINESS

Everything created by God contains a spark of holiness.

—*Baal Shem Tov*

Holiness toward God and justice toward man usually go together.

—*Philo*

If you sanctify yourself a little, you are sanctified a great deal.

—*Talmud*

HOME

Home means one's wife.

—*Talmud*

If you know you're going home, the trip is never too hard.

—*Chofetz Chaim*

A man must go out into the world to know how lovely is his own home.

—*Yiddish saying*

Anger in a home is like rottenness in a fruit.

—*Talmud*

HONESTY

Honesty is the precondition for genuine scientific and scholarly work.

—*Leo Baeck*

Honest dealing is possible only if one is not striving for wealth.

—*Rabbi Nahman of Bratslav*

HONOR

What is the virtuous path that a man should follow? Whatever brings honor to his Maker, and honor from his fellow man.

—*Judah Hanassi*

From honors, one cannot live.

—*Dutch Jewish saying*

No labor, however humble, dishonors a man.

—*Talmud*

I am below what people say, and above what they think.

—*Moses ibn Ezra*

A man should honor his father and mother as he honors God, for all three are partners in him.

—*Judah Hanassi*

HOPE

Deferred hope sickens the heart, but desire fulfilled is a tree of life.

—*Proverbs*

As long as a person breathes, he should not lose hope.

—*Talmud*

Man lives in hope.

—*Yiddish saying*

HOSPITALITY

Welcome everyone with joy.
                    —*Ethics of the Fathers*

Men like guests more than women do.
                              —*Talmud*

If you enter the city of the blind, cover your eyes.
                    —*Persian Jewish saying*

HUMILITY

Wisdom engenders humility.
                    —*Abraham ibn Ezra*

Be humble, so that you will not be humbled.
                              —*Talmud*

Be very humble, for man's destiny is the worm.

                    —*Ethics of the Fathers*

Always be humble, but not by bowing your head which is external humility. Real humility is internal and has its origin in wisdom.

—*Rabbi Nahman of Bratslav*

HUNGER

A timely quotation is like bread to the starving.

—*Rava*

The rich swell up from pride, the poor from hunger.

—*Shalom Aleichem*

Health? Very nice! But where will we get potatoes?

—*Yiddish saying*

The laborer's appetite works for him, for his hunger urges him on.

—*Proverbs*

HUSBAND

A husband's patience atones for all crimes.
—*Heinrich Heine*

A henpecked husband gets no relief in court.
—*Talmud*

When the husband is a rabbi, the wife is a *rebbitsen*. When he is a bath attendant, she is a bath attendant's wife.
—*Yiddish saying*

A faithless husband makes a wife faithless.
—*Talmud*

HYPOCRISY

Beware the man who has two faces and two hearts.
—*Moses ibn Ezra*

There are four groups of people who cannot see God's spirit: those who mock, hypocrites, slanderers, and liars.

—*Midrash*

An idolator worships one object, but there is no limit to the number of men whom a hypocrite worships.

—*Bahya ibn Pakuda*

IDEALISM

The twentieth-century ideals of America have been the ideals of the Jews for more than twenty centuries.

—*Louis D. Brandeis*

If I do not acquire ideals in my youth, when will I? Not in old age.

—*Maimonides*

Every dogma has its day, but ideals are eternal.

—*Israel Zangwill*

IDLENESS

Whoever does not work will suffer all his life.
—*Maimonides*

Idleness is the mother of famine.

—*Tobit*

Lazybones, go to the ant: study its ways and learn. Without leaders, officers, or rulers, it lays up its stores during the summer, gathers in its food at the harvest. How long will you lie there, lazybones? When will you wake up from your sleep? A bit more sleep, a bit more slumber, a bit more hugging yourself in bed, and poverty will come calling upon you.

—*Proverbs*

IGNORANCE

An ignorant man cannot be pious.

—*Hillel*

For the ignorant, old age is winter. For the wise, old age is the harvest season.

—*Hassidic saying*

The ignorant think less clearly as they age; scholars think more clearly as they grow older.

—*Talmud*

Do not mock the ignorant; you may be maligning your ancestors.

—*Wisdom of Sirach*

IMMORTALITY

The righteous live forever.

—*Wisdom of Sirach*

Upon death, the soul goes out of one door and enters another.

—*Baal Shem Tov*

INDEPENDENCE

Rather than become dependent, do work even if it is beneath you.

—*Talmud*

Whoever depends on his wife's earnings will not succeed.

—*Talmud*

Without moral and intellectual independence, there is no anchor for national independence.

—*David ben Gurion*

Make your Sabbath a weekday, but do not depend on others.

—*Rabbi Akiva*

INFLUENCE

To cause a man to sin is worse than murdering him.

—*Simeon bar Yochai*

A person who is charitable and just fills the world with kindness.

—*Talmud*

INGRATITUDE

Never insult your servants and do not stint in praising them, for the worst quality is ingratitude. Do not be ungrateful to animals, for riders who stick their spurs into horses will be punished.

—*Judah ben Samuel*

If you give people nuts, you'll get shells thrown at you.

—*Yemenite Jewish saying*

INTELLECT

Intelligence means a person who can see implications and arrive at conclusions.

—*Talmud*

Saichel (common sense) is a gift; intelligence is an acquisition.

—*Solomon ibn Gabirol*

Intellect is the dividing line between man and beast. It masters natural impulses and subdues passions.

—*Solomon ibn Gabirol*

ISRAEL

The Torah cannot assume perfection except in Israel.

—*Nahmanides*

No matter where I go, it is always to Israel.

—*Rabbi Nahman of Bratslav*

The (Western) Wall: The old mother crying for all of us, stubborn, loving, waiting for redemption. The ground on which I stand is Amen. I am afraid of indifference. Since Auschwitz my joys grieve, pleasures are mixed with vexations ... no security anywhere, anytime. The sun can be a nightmare, humanity infinitely worse than a beast. ... Once you have lived a moment at the Wall, you never go away. Jerusalem, you are not a shrine, a place of pilgrimage to which to come, and then depart. Let Jerusalem speak again to our people, to all people.

—*Abraham Joshua Heschel*

JEALOUSY

Jealousy in the heart makes the bones rot.
—*Proverbs*

The man who loves without jealousy does not truly love.

—*Zohar*

It's better for someone to be the object of jealousy, than of pity.

—*Moroccan Jewish saying*

You're jealous? Go out and ask for donations.
—*Dutch Jewish saying*

JEWS

We are a people, one people.
—*Theodor Herzl*

(The Jew) has made a marvelous fight in this world, in all the ages, and he has done so with his hands tied behind him.
—*Mark Twain*

The Jew is the emblem of eternity. He whom neither slaughter nor torture of thousands of years could destroy. . . . He who was the first to produce the oracles of God, he who has been for so long the guardian of prophecy, and transmitted it to the rest of the world—such a nation cannot be destroyed. The Jew is everlasting as eternity itself.
—*Leo Tolstoy*

The Jewish people is wise-hearted with the sorrows of every land.
—*Jessie Sampter*

The Jews, like the Greeks, were a unique fact in the development of man. . . . This particular race became the vehicle of new ideas.

—*Barbara Ward*

We have to look to Jewry, who were the first to believe that history itself has meaning and that progress, not repetition, is the law of life.

—*Barbara Ward*

JOY

Fulfill God's precepts joyfully, just as Israel accepted the Torah at Sinai with joy.

—*Judah Hanassi*

God is with the joyful man. He forsakes the sad man.

—*Rabbi Nahman of Bratslav*

Eat your bread with joy, drink your wine with a merry heart.

—*Ecclesiastes*

You can cage a bird but you can't make it sing.
—*French Jewish saying*

Joy comes with the morning.

—*Psalms*

JUDAISM

Judaism is the belief that all life should be sanctified and transfigured by religion. . . . Man is to humanize himself by conscious adherence to the moral law.

—*Claude Montefiore*

Israel's most cherished ideal is the universal brotherhood of mankind.

—*Samson Raphael Hirsch*

Judaism looks upon all human beings as children of one Father; thinks of them all as created in the image of God, and insists that a man be judged not by his religion, but his deeds.

—*Samuel Luzzatto*

JUDGE/JUDGMENT

The judge who passes sentence must fast on the day of execution.

—*Rabbi Akiva*

Do not judge your fellow man until you have stood in his place.

—*Hillel*

Judge a country's prosperity by its treatment of the aged.

—*Rabbi Nahman of Bratslav*

The man who accepts tradition without applying his own intelligence and judgment is like a blind person following others.

—*Bahya ibn Pakuda*

Judge a man not by the words of his mother, but from the comments of his neighbors.

—*Talmud*

Look at the end of the verse; do not judge half a passage.

—*B'ruriah*

JUSTICE

Give every man the benefit of the doubt.
—*Ethics of the Fathers*

Arbitrating is tempering justice with charity.
—*Rabbi Nahman of Bratslav*

What does the Lord require of you? Only to do justice, and to love goodness, and to walk humbly with God.

—*Micah*

KINDNESS

Every act of kindness that God performs for man should make him feel not proud, but more humble and unworthy.

—*Shneur Zalman*

The highest form of wisdom is kindness.
                                    —*Talmud*

Blessed is the man whose heart bears no malice.
                                    —*Baruch*

KNOWLEDGE

When wine enters, knowledge exits.
                                    —*Midrash*

He who increases knowledge, increases sorrow.
                                    —*Ecclesiastes*

No one is poor except one who lacks knowledge.
                                    —*Talmud*

Whoever wishes to know everything ages early.
                                    —*Yiddish saying*

LABOR

Only things acquired by hard labor and great struggle are of any value.

—Vilna Gaon

If you have to hire a laborer for a specialized job and one candidate can do only that work and another can also do others, hire the former.

—Judah ben Samuel

Man dies when he stops working.

—Talmud

Only he who worked before the Sabbath may dine on the Sabbath.

—Talmud

To earn a living can be as hard as parting the Red Sea.

—Talmud

LAUGHTER

God is the creator of laughter that is good.

—*Philo*

A fool raises his voice when he laughs, a wise man smiles quietly.

—*Wisdom of Sirach*

LAW

Whatever is hateful to you, do not do to your neighbor—that is the whole Law (Torah). All the rest is commentary. Now go and study.

—*Hillel*

The law of the state is the law.

—*Talmud*

Judaism is not identical with the law: it creates it. Judaism itself is not law. Judaism is—to be a Jew.

—*Franz Rosenzweig*

A student of laws who does not understand their meaning, or cannot explain their contradictions, is just a basket full of books.

—*Rashi*

LEADERSHIP

Leadership shortens life.

—*Talmud*

A wise man is a greater asset to a nation than a king.

—*Maimonides*

When a man can accept abuse with a smile, he is worthy of becoming a leader.
—*Rabbi Nahman of Bratslav*

Too many captains will sink a ship.
—*Talmud*

LEARNING

Three things can be learned from a railroad: if you are one minute late, you miss it; the slightest deflection from the rails leads to disaster; and a passenger without a ticket may expect punishment.

—*Israel Salanter*

He who does not learn forfeits his life.

—*Hillel*

The advancement of learning is the highest commandment.

—*Maimonides*

No person is too old to learn.

—*French Jewish saying*

A man should never stop learning, even on his last day.

—*Maimonides*

A shy person does not learn.

—*Ethics of the Fathers*

LEGEND

To him who knows how to read the legend, it conveys more truth than the chronicle.

—*Martin Buber*

LIAR

Lordly words are not suitable for a fool, much less are lying words for a lord.

—*Proverbs*

To some people, lying is a profession.

—*Moses Luzzatto*

A person who has no confidence speaks lies; a liar has no confidence.

—*Rabbi Nahman of Bratslav*

LIFE

Don't worry about tomorrow. Who knows what may happen to you today?

—Talmud

Life is the highest good, and death the worst evil.

—Heinrich Heine

All creatures pass over a frail bridge, connecting life with death. Life is its entrance, death its exit.

—Bahya ibn Pakuda

Life is a series of vexations and pains, and sleepless nights are the common lot.

—Vilna Gaon

LIGHT

The world is full of radiant, wonderful, and elevating secrets, and it is only the small hand held up before our eyes which prevents us from seeing the light.

—*Baal Shem Tov*

A light for one is a light for one hundred.

—*Talmud*

LITERATURE

A wise man without a book is like an artisan without tools.

—*Moroccan Jewish saying*

Teachers die, but books live on.

—*Dutch Jewish saying*

LOGIC

Wisdom is like gold ore in the ground mixed with sand and rock: logic is the mercury used to extract the gold.

—Moses ibn Ezra

We cannot learn everything from "general principles"—there may be exceptions.

—Talmud

LONELINESS

Pity the outsider even if he is rich.

—Yemenite Jewish saying

Between bad company and loneliness, the latter is preferable.

—Sephardic saying

A man who thinks he can live without other people is wrong, and a man who thinks others cannot live without him is even more wrong.

—Hassidic saying

LOVE

Accept your afflictions with love and joy.
                    —*Eleazar ben Judah of Worms*

Whether a man really loves God can be determined by his love for his fellow man.
                    —*Rabbi Levi Isaac of Berdichev*

To obey out of love is better than to obey out of fear.

                                        —*Rashi*

A woman prefers poverty with love to wealth without love.

                                    —*Talmud*

Love makes one blind and deaf.
                    —*Solomon ibn Gabirol*

Love is the voice of God.

                            —*Grace Aquilar*

A woman that is loved always has success.

—*Vicki Baum*

LOYALTY

Loyalty will gain you entry to the sultan's house.

—*Tunisian Jewish saying*

Old love does not rust.

—*Yiddish saying*

If you eat someone's cake, you must also eat his lentils.

—*Dutch Jewish saying*

LUCK

If you have luck, even your ox will calve.

—*Yiddish saying*

Mourn for the man who does not know his good fortune.

—*Talmud*

Luck is better than wisdom.
—*French Jewish saying*

A fool has luck.
—*German Jewish saying*

LUST

Lust should be stifled, for it does not lead to truth.
—*Moses ibn Ezra*

Lust and reason are enemies.
—*Solomon ibn Gabirol*

A lecherous old man is disgusting.
—*Talmud*

The licentious age early.
—*Talmud*

MAN

I am a Jew, because for Israel man is not created—men are creating him.

—*Edmond Fleg*

Many a man who does not fear God wraps himself in a prayer shawl.

—*Abraham ibn Ezra*

Man is free in his imagination, but bound by his reason.

—*Israel Salanter*

Where there are no men, try to be a man.

—*Hillel*

What is man that Thou art mindful of him? Yet, Thou hast made him but a little lower than the angels.

—*Psalms*

MANKIND

Man's creed is that he believes in God and therefore in mankind, but not that he believes in a creed.

—*Leo Baeck*

Men who are ruled by reason desire nothing for themselves which they would not wish for all mankind.

—*Baruch Spinoza*

MANNERS

The test of good manners is to be patient with bad ones.

—*Solomon ibn Gabirol*

Manners provide the lubrication without which frictions would develop.

—*Edgar Magnin*

If you empty a cup of wine in one gulp, you are a drunkard.

—*Talmud*

There is no better index to intelligence than the way one behaves at the table.

—*Solomon ibn Gabirol*

MARRIAGE

One wife is enough for any man.

—*Abraham ibn Ezra*

He who remains unmarried impairs the divine image.

—*Rabbi Akiva*

Every bride is beautiful and graceful.

—*Hillel*

Whoever marries for money will have unworthy children.

—*Talmud*

No marriage contract is made without a quarrel.

—*Talmud*

Being an old maid is like death by drowning: a really delightful sensation, after you cease to struggle.

—*Edna Ferber*

MEALS

Three people who dine together and do not exchange words of Torah are considered as though they have eaten an idolatrous sacrifice.

—*Simeon bar Yochai*

It is better to take food into the mouth than to take worries into the heart.

—*Yiddish saying*

Whoever goes to bed hungry will wake up sleepless.

—*Yiddish saying*

MEDICINE

God is the best physician.
—*German Jewish saying*

A doctor's mistake is covered up by the earth.
—*Sephardic saying*

MEEKNESS

Meekness is the greatest of virtues.
—*Talmud*

Be very meek, for man's destiny is the worm.
—*Ethics of the Fathers*

Too meek is half-proud. It is better to be humble with the meek than share spoils with the proud.

—*Proverbs*

MELANCHOLY

An orphan weeps. A bitter person talks a lot.
—Yiddish saying

Do not sigh, for your enemy will hear and rejoice.
—Yemenite Jewish saying

When you laugh, everyone sees. When you cry, not one person sees.
—Yiddish saying

How lovely is the sun after rain, and how lovely is laughter after sorrow.
—Tunisian Jewish saying

MEMORY

Remember famine in a time of plenty, and poverty and want in a season of prosperity.
—Wisdom of Sirach

The memory of the righteous shall be for a blessing.

—*Proverbs*

To remember well is not necessarily a sign of wisdom.

—*Samuel Luzzatto*

MERCY

He who has mercy on the cruel will in the end behave cruelly to the merciful.

—*Simeon ben Lakish*

He who asks mercy for another, while he himself is in need, will be answered first.

—*Talmud*

The mercy of the wicked is cruel.

—*Proverbs*

MEN

Women want to be married more than men do.

—*Talmud*

The ideal man has the strength of men and the compassion of women.

—*Zohar*

It is easier to placate a man than a woman: The first man came from soft dust, but the first woman was created from hard bone.

—*Talmud*

MIND

When your mind is not at ease, don't pray.

—*Abba Aricha*

The mind of each person is as individual as his face.

—*Talmud*

There is no state of mind, however simple, that does not change every minute.

—*Henri Bergson*

More than all that you guard, guard your mind, for it is the source of life.

—*Proverbs*

A closed mind is a dying mind.

—*Edna Ferber*

MIRACLE

Hope for a miracle, but don't rely on it.

—*Talmud*

A miracle cannot prove what is impossible; it is helpful only as confirmation of what is possible.

—*Maimonides*

MISER

Seeking charity from a miser is like fishing in the desert.

—*Solomon ibn Gabirol*

Miserliness does not enrich a person; benevolence does not impoverish anyone.

—*Yiddish saying*

MISFORTUNE

To believe that no misfortune will befall you is like not wishing to live; misfortunes are a necessary part of this world.

—*Solomon ibn Gabirol*

One day's happiness makes misfortunes forgotten—one day's misfortune makes a person forget past joys.

—*Wisdom of Sirach*

MODERATION

There are eight things of which a little is good, and too much is bad: travel, mating, wealth, work, wine, sleep, spiced drinks, and medicine.

—Talmud

Moderation prolongs life.

—Wisdom of Sirach

Excessive sitting aggravates hemorrhoids; excessive standing strains the heart; too much walking injures the eyes. Divide your time among the three.

—Talmud

MODESTY

Modesty is an index to nobility.

—Moses ibn Ezra

Modesty is meekness and wisdom combined.

—Solomon ibn Gabirol

MONEY

As a general rule, nobody has money who ought to have it.

—*Benjamin Disraeli*

When death calls a person to appear before his Maker, money—which people love—cannot go along.

—*Talmud*

One who saves his money is worth more than one who earns it.

—*Yiddish saying*

Money rules the world.

—*Dutch Jewish saying*

Money paves a path through the sea.

—*Moroccan Jewish saying*

A full pocket will heal the sick.

—*Italian Jewish saying*

MORALITY

Morality will conquer war even as it has conquered human sacrifice, slavery, feuds, head-hunting, and cannibalism.

—*Max Nordau*

Morality is more important than learning.

—*Talmud*

Judaism is not merely ethical, but ethics is its essence.

—*Leo Baeck*

MOTHER

There is no bad mother and no good death.

—*Yiddish saying*

Adam was the luckiest man—he had no mother-in-law.

—*Shalom Aleichem*

A modest woman has good children.
—*Rabbi Nahman of Bratslav*

Like the mother, so is the daughter.
—*Ezekiel*

MOURNING

It is better to visit a house of mourning than go to a house of feasting.
—*Ecclesiastes*

Whoever does not patiently subdue his mourning will prolong his grief.
—*Solomon ibn Gabirol*

MOUTH

Speak not one thing with your mouth and another with your heart.
—*Abbaye*

Nature has given us two ears, but only one mouth.
—*Benjamin Disraeli*

Give your ear to all, your hand to a friend, but your mouth only to your wife.

—*Yiddish saying*

MURDER

Whoever destroys a single life is as guilty as though he has destroyed the whole world. Whoever saves a single life, it is as though he saved the whole world.

—*Talmud*

If a man kills a thief, it is not murder. A thief is like a person who has been dead from the start.

—*Rashi*

NAME

No monument sheds such glory as an untarnished name.

—*Eleazar ben Judah of Worms*

There are three crowns: Torah, Priesthood, Royalty. The crown of a good name is superior to them all.

—*Simeon bar Yochai*

NATION

Nationalism is an infantile sickness. It is the measles of the human race.

—*Albert Einstein*

Israel, you are a lucky people. When you obey God's will, no nation can rule over you. But when you do not obey His will, then you are at the mercy of every people, however low-born.

—*Johanan ben Zakkai*

A nationality without an historical language, without a sacred literature, is a mere gypsy camp.

—*Solomon Schechter*

NATURE

The power of nature is the power of God.
> —*Baruch Spinoza*

While the earth remains, seeding time and harvest, cold and heat, summer and winter, and day and night, will not cease.
> —*Genesis*

Don't ask God to change the laws of nature for you.
> —*Rabbi Nahman of Bratslav*

NECESSITY

Necessity can break iron.

—*Yiddish saying*

NEIGHBOR

"Love your neighbor as yourself" is the great principle of the Torah.

—*Rabbi Akiva*

If you seek to lead your neighbor in the right path, you must do so out of love.

—*Baal Shem Tov*

Better a nearby neighbor than a far-off brother.

—*Proverbs*

NOBILITY

What is the noblest pedigree? Loving-kindness.

—*Solomon ibn Gabirol*

He is noble who both feels and acts nobly.

—*Heinrich Heine*

There is no pedigree as noble as virtue and no heritage equal to honor.

—*Maimonides*

OATH

"No" is an oath. "Yes" is an oath.

—*Talmud*

OBLIGATION

No man may buy a beast, an animal, or a bird until he provides it with food.

—*Talmud*

I did not find the world desolate when I entered it. My fathers planted for me before I arrived, so do I plant for those who come after me.

—*Talmud*

OCCUPATION

Whoever does not teach his son a trade, teaches him robbery.

—*Tosefta (Kiddushin)*

Master a trade, and God will provide.
—*Ecclesiastes Rabbah*

OLD AGE

Do not dishonor the old—we shall be numbered among them.

—*Wisdom of Sirach*

An old man in the house is a burden, but an old woman is a treasure.

—*Talmud*

OPINION

From your opinion of others, we know the opinion of you.

—*Moses ibn Ezra*

Intelligent people must examine all opinions.

—*Maimonides*

There is no arguing about people's tastes.

—*Israeli saying*

OPPORTUNITY

Next to knowing when to seize an opportunity, the next important thing in life is to know when to forego an advantage.

—*Benjamin Disraeli*

One must bless the new moon when she is visible in the sky.

—*French Jewish saying*

OPTIMISM

It is better to display a smiling face than offer someone milk.

—*Talmud*

ORPHAN

Whoever rears an orphan, it is as though he has brought him into the world.

—*Talmud*

PAIN

Whom the Lord loves, He crushes with pain.

—*Talmud*

Never to have had pain is not to have been human.

—*Yiddish saying*

PARADISE

Those who feel true shame will go to the Garden of Eden.

—*Ethics of the Fathers*

My thoughts form an Eden in my heart.
—*Judah Halevi*

PARENTS

To honor parents is even more important than to honor God.

—*Simeon bar Yochai*

Let us be grateful to our parents, for had they not been tempted, we would not be here.
—*Talmud*

When a father gives to his son, they both laugh. When a son gives to his father, they both weep.

—*Yiddish saying*

Hear, my son, the instruction of your father, and do not forsake the teaching of your mother.

—*Proverbs*

PASSION

Do not be a slave to your passions lest they consume your strength like a bull.

—*Wisdom of Sirach*

It is easier for an apathetic man to be stirred to pleasure than for a man afire with passion to curb his lusts.

—*Maimonides*

PAST

The past is our cradle, not our prison; there is danger as well as appeal in its glamour. The past is an interpretation, not imitation, for continuation, not repetition.

—*Israel Zangwill*

PATIENCE

Patience is half of wisdom.
—*Sephardic saying*

There are two main human sins from which all the others stem—impatience and indolence.
—*Franz Kafka*

Nothing reduces misfortune like patience.
—*Solomon ibn Gabirol*

PEACE

God is present whenever a peace treaty is signed.
—*Rabbi Nahman of Bratslav*

Be a disciple of Aaron, loving peace and pursuing peace, loving your fellow man and attracting him to the study of Torah.

—*Hillel*

Peace, like charity, begins at home.
—*Itzhak ben Zvi*

Where there is no peace, prayers are not accepted.

—*Rabbi Nahman of Bratslav*

PEDAGOGY

The bad-tempered cannot teach.

—*Hillel*

Open your lesson with a joke; let your students laugh a little. Then become serious.

—*Talmud*

If there are more than twenty-five children in a school for young children, hire an assistant.

—*Talmud*

PEOPLE

The *Privileged* and the *People* form two nations.

—*Benjamin Disraeli*

Where there is no vision, the people perish.

—*Proverbs*

Listen to the voice of the people.

—*Samuel I*

PERFECTION

Man is capable of perfection because of the power of reason, given to him by God.

—*Maimonides*

The desire to seek perfection, to overcome the physical, and find harmony of being has been the affirmative note in Jewish history.

—*Chaim Weizmann*

PERSEVERANCE

Whoever persists in knocking will succeed in entering.

—*Moses ibn Ezra*

A righteous man falls seven times, and rises up again.

—*Proverbs*

PESSIMISM

Utter futility! Utter futility! All is futility!
—*Ecclesiastes*

April Fool is a joke—it is repeated 365 times a year.

—*Shalom Aleichem*

Don't worry about tomorrow. Who knows what will happen to you today?

—*Talmud*

PIETY

Beware of a pious fool, and of a wise sinner.
—*Solomon ibn Gabirol*

He who is pious and learned is like an artist with his tools, ready and at hand.

—*Johanan ben Zakkai*

PLEASURE

Each individual will be called to account in the hereafter for every pleasure he declined without sufficient cause.

—*Abba Aricha*

Pleasures are manifestations of God's name.

—*Baal Shem Tov*

POVERTY

You cannot compare the man who has bread with the man who has not.

—*Talmud*

He who scorns the poor insults the Lord. He who rejoices at their misfortune will not go unpunished.

—*Proverbs*

Poverty outweighs all other troubles.

—*Exodus Rabbah*

Poverty is no disgrace; neither is it an honor.
—*Yiddish saying*

Do not be impoverished from feasting on borrowed money when your own purse is empty.
—*Wisdom of Sirach*

No one is so poor as an ignorant person.
—*Talmud*

POWER

A tiny fly can choke a big man.
—*Solomon ibn Gabirol*

Put not your trust in princes.

—*Psalms*

Power buries those who wield it.

—*Talmud*

The lust for power is not rooted in strength, but in weakness.

—*Erich Fromm*

PRAISE

Let another man praise you, and not your own mouth.

—*Proverbs*

PRAYER

In prayer, always associate yourself with the congregation and say, "*Our* God, lead *us*."

—*Abbaye*

It is better to pray at home, for in the synagogue it is impossible to escape envy, and hearing idle talk.

—*Vilna Gaon*

A life of isolation, devoted only to prayer and meditation, is not Jewish.

—*Samson Raphael Hirsch*

Proper praying is like a man who wanders through a field gathering flowers—one by one, until they make a beautiful bouquet. In the same manner, a man must gather each letter, each syllable, to form them into the words of prayer.

—*Rabbi Nahman of Bratslav*

PRIDE

A proud man is not loved even in his own home.

—*Talmud*

The proud man cannot humble himself to learn wisdom.

—*Saadiah Gaon*

A proud man never praises anyone.

—*Zohar*

PROMISE

Vote for the man who promises least; he will be the least disappointing.

—*Bernard Baruch*

A promise unkept leads to a bad life.
                                    —*Yiddish saying*

Evening promises are like butter: morning comes, and it's all melted.
                                    —*Moroccan Jewish saying*

PROVERBS

A proverb without wisdom is like a body without a foot.
                                    —*Abraham ibn Ezra*

A proverb has three characteristics: few words, good sense, a fine image.
                                    —*Moses ibn Ezra*

PRUDENCE

A man should not hide all his money in one place.
                                    —*Genesis Rabbah*

The simpleton trusts everything. The wise man heeds his steps.

—*Proverbs*

As long as I do not speak a word, I am its master. Once I say it, I am its slave.
—*Solomon ibn Gabirol*

Discretion shall preserve you.

—*Proverbs*

Open not your heart to every man.
—*Wisdom of Sirach*

PUBLICITY

What is improper in public is forbidden in secret.

—*Abba Aricha*

Judaism need not be advertised; Judaism needs to be taught.

—*Solomon Schechter*

Hidden wisdom and concealed treasure: what profit is there in either?

—*Wisdom of Sirach*

A man's service of God is sincere when he wants no publicity for it.

—*Rabbi Nahman of Bratslav*

PUNISHMENT

To punish a student, use a shoe lace.

—*Talmud*

Order cannot be secured merely through fear of punishment. It is hazardous to discourage thought, hope and imagination. Fear breeds repression; repression breeds hate; hate menaces stable government.

—*Louis D. Brandeis*

A soothing tongue is a tree of life, but wild words can break the spirit.

—*Proverbs*

QUANTITY

Better is a little, with the fear of the Lord, than great treasure with its accompanying turmoil.

—*Proverbs*

In creative work, never consider quantity. Obadiah consists of one chapter, yet it found its place in the Bible.

—*Chaim Nahman Bialik*

To sum up the trend of Jewish history, I should answer in three words: quality versus quantity. All down the years, from Joshua to today, we have been the few withstanding the many.

—*David ben Gurion*

QUARREL

Keep far from strife, and sin will keep far from you.

—*Wisdom of Sirach*

Dissension in a house will lead to its destruction.
—*Talmud*

A quarrelsome man deserves no answers.
—*Rabbi Nahman of Bratslav*

When two men quarrel, the one who yields first displays the nobler character.
—*Talmud*

QUESTION

We are encompassed by questions, to which only awe can respond.
—*Leo Baeck*

The fool wonders, the wise man asks.
—*Benjamin Disraeli*

Asking questions is man's finest quality.
—*Solomon ibn Gabirol*

RAIN

When do Jews and Gentiles rejoice together?
When it rains.

—*Talmud*

Rain is greater than the resurrection since that
is only for the righteous. Rain is for everyone.

—*Talmud*

RANK

Take your place a little below your rank until
you are asked to move up. It is better to be told
to "come up" higher than "move down."

—*Rabbi Akiva*

A boor should not ride the king's horse.

—*Yiddish saying*

REASON

Reason has long since decided that God needs nothing, but that all things need Him.

—*Saadiah Gaon*

Any interpretation that conforms to reason must be correct.

—*Saadiah Gaon*

Reason is the angel that mediates between God and man.

—*Abraham ibn Ezra*

We have no doctrines that are contrary to reason. We added nothing to natural religion except commandments and statutes. But the fundamental tenets of our religion rest on the foundation of reason.

—*Moses Mendelssohn*

REBUKE

Do not reject the discipline of the Lord, my son, do not abhor His rebuke. For whom the Lord loves, He rebukes, as a father the son whom he favors.

—Proverbs

My friend is one who will tell me my faults in private.

—Moses ibn Ezra

REDEMPTION

The Jew carries the burden of an unredeemed world. He cannot concede that redemption is an accomplished fact, for he knows it is not so.

—Martin Buber

Man's good deeds are single acts in the long drama of redemption.

—Abraham Joshua Heschel

RELATIVES

Never do business with your relations.

—*Hai Gaon*

Whoever gossips about his relatives has no luck and no blessing.

—*Dutch Jewish saying*

RELIGION

Religion may be the concern of a people, but it must never become the concern of the state.

—*Leo Baeck*

People whose religion begins and ends with worship and ritual practices are like soldiers forever maneuvering, but never getting into action.

—*Mordecai Kaplan*

My religiosity consists in a humble admiration of the infinitely superior spirit that reveals itself in the little that, with our weak and transitory understanding, we can comprehend of reality. Morality is of the highest importance, but for us, not for God.

—*Albert Einstein*

REPENTANCE

Repentance prolongs a man's life.

—*Talmud*

Great is repentance; it turns sins into incentives for correct conduct.

—*Simeon ben Lakish*

Great is repentance because it brings the human being close to the Divine Presence. Yesterday, when a person sinned, he was hated before God, disgusting and distant, an abomination. Today, he is beloved, sweet, near, a precious friend. Yesterday a person was separated from God. Today he cleaves to the Divine Presence.

—*Maimonides*

REPUTATION

Beauty wanes, but a good name endures.

—*Ahikar*

In your community, your name counts. In another town, your clothes matter.

—*Talmud*

A good name is more valuable than a velvet garment.

—*Moroccan Jewish saying*

RESPECT

If you are truly a Jew, you will be respected because of it, not in spite of it.

—*Samson Raphael Hirsch*

Whoever does not respect you, insults you.

—*Moroccan Jewish saying*

RESPONSIBILITY

All men are responsible for one another.
                                    —*Talmud*

One should not send a cat to deliver cream.
                                    —*Yiddish saying*

Do not hold a man responsible for what he says in his distress.
                                    —*Talmud*

REST

Resting is not worthwhile unless it follows labor.
                                    —*Saadiah Gaon*

Rest is a state of peace, between man and nature. Work is a symbol of conflict and discord; rest is an expression of dignity, peace and freedom.
                                    —*Erich Fromm*

RETRIBUTION

Those who sow the wind will reap the whirlwind.

—*Hosea*

I believe with perfect faith that the Creator rewards those who keep His commandments and punishes those who transgress them.

—*Maimonides*

Whoever digs a pit will fall into it. He who rolls a stone, it will come back upon him.

—*Proverbs*

REVENGE

You shall not take vengeance, nor bear a grudge.

—*Leviticus*

Whoever takes revenge destroys his own home.

—*Talmud*

He avenged himself on fleas, and burned up his bed.

—*Yiddish saying*

REWARD

The way you sow, so shall you reap.

—*Yemenite Jewish saying*

An animal's end is slaughter. A thief's end is hanging.

—*Yiddish saying*

Perform good deeds; you will not regret them.

—*Moroccan Jewish saying*

The way you prepare the bed, so shall you sleep.

—*Yiddish saying*

RICHES

Whoever trusts in his wealth will fall.
—*Proverbs*

Riches have led astray the hearts of princes.
—*Bahya ibn Pakuda*

Who loves silver cannot be satisfied with silver.

—*Ecclesiastes*

God loves the poor, and helps the rich.
—*Yiddish saying*

In the eyes of God, the rich and poor are equal.

—*German Jewish saying*

RIGHTEOUS

In the future world there will be no eating, drinking, propagation, business, jealousy, hatred, or compensation, but the righteous will sit with crowns on their heads, enjoying the brilliance of the Divine Presence.

—*Abba Aricha*

God performs signs and wonders through the righteous even as He did formerly for the prophets.

—*Hai Gaon*

Better a little with righteousness than a great deal with injustice.

—*Proverbs*

RULE

As a rule, men love one another—from a distance.

—*Shalom Aleichem*

The high destiny of the individual is to serve rather than to rule.

—*Albert Einstein*

An exception casts light on a rule.

—*Numbers Rabbah*

RUMOR

A talkative man is dreaded, and a man who speaks rashly is hated.

—*Wisdom of Sirach*

Good tidings can be heard from afar.

—*Yiddish saying*

Do not rejoice on hearing a bad rumor.

—*Yemenite Jewish saying*

People talk about something, until it comes to pass.

—*German Jewish saying*

SABBATH

Jerusalem was destroyed because it had desecrated the Sabbath.

—Talmud

More than Israel kept the Sabbath, the Sabbath kept Israel.

—Ahad Ha'am

Sabbath is the anticipation of the messianic time, just as the messianic period is called the time of "continuous Sabbath."

—Erich Fromm

SADNESS

An orphan weeps a lot. A bitter person talks a lot.

—Yiddish saying

Don't sigh; if your enemy hears, he'll rejoice.
—Yemenite Jewish saying

SAGES

To see a sage die is like seeing a holy scroll burn.

—*Talmud*

SCHOLAR

If you must, sell everything and marry your daughter to a scholar.

—*Talmud*

Jerusalem was destroyed for not respecting scholars.

—*Talmud*

Better make friends with an ignoramus who is liberal with his money and of a pleasing disposition than with a scholar who is mean and irascible.

—*Judah ben Samuel*

SCIENCE

Science without religion is lame. Religion without science is blame.

—*Albert Einstein*

SECRET

Your secret is your prisoner. Once you reveal it, you become its slave.

—*Solomon ibn Gabirol*

What three people know is no secret.

—*Yiddish saying*

The secrets of people are as varied as their faces.

—*Talmud*

SELF

Promote yourself, but do not demote another.
—*Israel Salanter*

If I am not concerned for myself, who will be for me? But if I am only for myself, what good am I? And if now is not the time [to act], when will it be?

—*Hillel*

Ten enemies cannot hurt a man as much as he hurts himself.
—*Yiddish saying*

First, become a blessing to yourself so that you may be a blessing to others.
—*Samson Raphael Hirsch*

Without being and remaining oneself, there is no love.

—*Martin Buber*

There is no room for God in a person who is full of himself.

—*Baal Shem Tov*

SELFISHNESS

If my child and I have eaten, you can clear the table.

—Moroccan Jewish saying

Pay me what you owe me. As for my debt to you, let's talk.

—Sephardic saying

Selfishness is the only real atheism. Aspiration and unselfishness, the only real religion.

—Israel Zangwill

An ignoramus believes the whole world exists only for him. If anything happens to him contrary to his expectations, he concludes the whole world is evil.

—Maimonides

SENSITIVITY

Do not show gallows to a man sentenced to hang.

—*Sephardic saying*

Do not sprinkle salt on a wound.

—*Yiddish saying*

Speak to a man in language he understands. Do not use literary words to the uneducated, nor vulgar terms to the learned.

—*Zohar*

SEX

Jews were too busy having children to bother with sex.

—*Maurice Samuel*

When passion burns within you, remember that it was given to you for a good purpose.

—*Hassidic saying*

SHAME

Do not enter into a learned discussion with your guests unless you are assured of their ability, so as not to put them to shame.

—*Judah ben Samuel*

Do not rebuke your fellow man so as not to shame him in public.

—*Rashi*

Humiliation is worse than physical pain.

—*Talmud*

Since dishonor is constant with a liar, he is always accompanied by shame.

—*Wisdom of Sirach*

SIGHT

A small coin before one's eyes hides everything from sight.

—*Israel Salanter*

SILENCE

If a word is worth one shekel, silence is worth two.

—*Talmud*

Silence is the only successful substitute for brains.

—*Maurice Samuel*

I can better retract what I did not say than what I did.

—*Solomon ibn Gabirol*

SIN

A person whose sins are greater than his merits will immediately die in his wickedness.

—*Maimonides*

A little sin becomes a big sin when committed by a big man.

—*Abraham ibn Ezra*

It is forbidden to observe a commandment by committing a sin.

—*Simeon bar Yochai*

Pride is the reservoir of sin.

—*Wisdom of Sirach*

Contemplate three things and you will avoid sin: Above you in heaven is an eye that sees, an ear that hears, and all your deeds are faithfully recorded.

—*Judah Hanassi*

Do not pray that sinners die, but [rather] that they repent.

—*B'ruriah*

SLANDER

Who shall reside in Thy tabernacle? He that has no slander on his lips.

—Psalms

There is no cure for a slanderer.

—Talmud

A fickle man sows discord, and a whisperer separates friends.

—Proverbs

Slander is worse than weapons: weapons injure from near, slander injures from afar.

—Talmud

SMUGNESS

Self-complacency is the companion of ignorance.

—*Solomon Schechter*

If a man, after prayer, is proud or self-satisfied, let him know that he has prayed not to God, but to himself.

—*Baal Shem Tov*

If you are completely free of sin, I am apprehensive of something in you worse than sin—haughtiness and pride.

—*Bahya ibn Pakuda*

SOLITUDE

Even in paradise, it is not good to be alone.

—*Yiddish saying*

The right to be alone [is] the most comprehensive of rights, and the right most valued by civilized men.

—*Louis D. Brandeis*

Woe to him who is alone when he falls.
—*Ecclesiastes*

Don't pity me if I am poor, but only if I am alone.
—*Sephardic saying*

Pity the stranger, even if he is rich.
—*Yemenite Jewish saying*

SON

A wise son makes his father glad; a foolish son is the grief of his mother.
—*Proverbs*

The only time a son should disobey his father is if the father tells him to commit a sin.
—*Talmud*

He who spares the rod hates his son.
—*Proverbs*

Apples don't fall from a pear tree.
—*French Jewish saying*

SPEECH

Be liberal with your wealth, not with your words.

—*Bahya ibn Pakuda*

Gentle speech multiplies friends.

—*Wisdom of Sirach*

Speech is a God-given boon peculiar to man, and must not be used for anything debasing.

—*Maimonides*

Whoever does not refrain from speaking, others will quiet him.

—*Persian Jewish saying*

What is lofty can be said in any language. What is mean should be said in none.

—*Maimonides*

Do not speak one way with your mouth, and another with your heart.

—*Abbaye*

SPIRITUAL

Pray for the suppression of evil, but never for one's own material well-being, for a separating veil arises if one admits the material into the spiritual.

—*Baal Shem Tov*

Wisdom is to the soul as food is to the body.

—*Abraham ibn Ezra*

STEALING

Stealing leads to poverty.

—*Iraqi Jewish saying*

Whoever steals an egg will steal a cow.

—*Tunisian Jewish saying*

Diplomacy is the art of dealing with thieves.

—*Theodor Herzl*

Guard your money, and don't suspect your neighbor.

—*Bokharan Jewish saying*

Whoever watches his house will discov that his neighbor is not a thief.

—*Moroccan Jewish sayir*

STRANGER

You shall love the stranger as yourself.

—*Leviticus*

It is hard to eat bread at a stranger's table.

—*Talmud*

A stranger is like a blind man.

—*Yemenite Jewish saying*

STRENGTH

The big fish eats the small one.

—*Sephardic saying*

A person does not fall because he is weak, but because he thinks he is strong.

—*Yiddish saying*

Be strong and of good courage!

—*Joshua*

When a stone hits glass, the glass breaks. When glass hits a stone, the glass breaks.

—*Persian Jewish saying*

What can a fist do against someone whom God gave strength?

—*Moroccan Jewish saying*

STUDENT/STUDY

I have learned much from my teachers, more from my colleagues, but most from my students.

—*Judah Hanassi*

One may not interrupt one's study of *Halachah* [Jewish religious law] for prayer.

—*Shneur Zalman*

The main thing is not to study, but to do.

—*Ethics of the Fathers*

Don't say "I'll study when I have time," because you may never have time.

—*Hillel*

SUCCESS

Try not to become a man of success, but rather try to become a man of value.

—*Albert Einstein*

From success to failure is one step. From failure to success is a long road.

—*Yiddish saying*

So long as everything is working well we're regarded as sages.

—*French Jewish saying*

Every man has the right to be conceited, until he is successful.

—*Benjamin Disraeli*

SUFFERING

I am a Jew because in every place where suffering weeps, the Jew weeps.

—*Edmond Fleg*

Suffering, consciously experienced and mastered, teaches us wisdom.

—*Theodore Reik*

If you want to live in this world, get yourself a heart that can endure suffering.

—*Leviticus Rabbah*

God tests the righteous.

—*Sephardic saying*

Whoever God loves, He punishes.

—*Dutch Jewish saying*

SUPERSTITION

Better a superstitious believer than a rationalistic unbeliever.

—*Rabbi Nahman of Bratslav*

SYMPATHY

My sympathies are with those Jews who are working for a revival of a Jewish state in Palestine. My sympathy with the Zionist movement rests primarily upon the noble idealism which underlies it.

—*Louis D. Brandeis*

SYNAGOGUE

One should run to synagogue.

—*Abbaye*

Synagogues and houses of study are Israel's fortresses.

—*Simeon bar Yochai*

Shuls are what we call our synagogues, and that is what they should be: schools for the grownups.
—*Samson Raphael Hirsch*

TALENT

To be a successful businessman, you must have remarkable talents; and if you have such talents, why waste them on business?
—*Israel Salanter*

TASTE

Before you taste anything, recite a blessing.
—*Rabbi Akiva*

Some prefer vinegar, and some prefer wine.
—*Talmud*

Every mouth prefers its own soup.
—*Sephardic saying*

There is just no debating about taste or smell.
—*Israeli saying*

TEACHER

More than the calf wants to suck, the cow wants to suckle—i.e., the teacher wants to teach more than the pupil wants to learn.

—Rabbi Akiva

Be sure to ask your teacher his reasons and his sources.

—Rashi

He who teaches a child, it is as though he created it.

—Talmud

Irascible people should not teach.

—Hillel

Turn to books only when you have no teacher.

—Moses ibn Ezra

Teachers learn from their students' discussions.

—Rashi

Get yourself a teacher, acquire a friend, and judge everyone charitably.

—*Ethics of the Fathers*

TEARS

Tears do not wipe out debts.

—*Yiddish saying*

There is no gate that tears cannot penetrate.

—*Zohar*

Those who sow in tears, will reap in song.

—*Psalms*

TEMPER

If a man can't control his temper, how can he control other people?

—*Solomon ibn Gabirol*

Whoever spares his words has true wisdom; he who holds his temper is a man of wisdom.

—*Proverbs*

TEMPTATION

Do not put yourself in the path of temptation—even King David could not resist it.

—*Talmud*

A man without a wife has no defense against temptation.

—*Talmud*

THOUGHT

The pure of heart find new thoughts whenever they meditate.

—*Rabbi Nahman of Bratslav*

A humble man walks on earth; his thoughts reach up to the heavens.

—*Samuel Hanagid*

It is better to talk to a woman and think of God, than talk to God and think of a woman.

—*Yiddish saying*

TIME

There is a time to love and a time to hate, a time to rejoice and a time to weep.

—*Ecclesiastes*

The Sabbath is an oasis in time.

—*Abraham Joshua Heschel*

When the time comes for you to live, there aren't enough years.

—*Yiddish saying*

Time is the same for pauper and priest.

—*Talmud*

Time teaches more than all our ills.

—*Benjamin Disraeli*

TOMORROW

Eat and drink for tomorrow we die.

—*Isaiah*

Boast not of tomorrow, for you know not what a day may bring.

—*Proverbs*

TONGUE

The tongue's sin weighs as much as all other sins together.

—*Vilna Gaon*

Let your tongue be imprisoned in your mouth.

—*Hai Gaon*

The tongue is the heart's pen and the mind's messenger.

—*Bahya ibn Pakuda*

The worst of men is he whose tongue is stronger than his mind.

—*Moses ibn Ezra*

TORAH

The more Torah, the more life. The more study, the more wisdom. The more counsel, the more discernment. The more charity, the more peace.

—*Hillel*

Like rain, the Torah nourishes useful plants and poisonous weeds.

—*Vilna Gaon*

If you have learned much Torah, do not boast of it, for it was for that purpose that you were born.

—*Johanan ben Zakkai*

To interpret the Torah properly we must remember that the whole of it is more than the sum of its parts.

—*Mordecai Kaplan*

Whoever studies Torah for its own sake merits many things: The whole world is indebted to him, he is called friend, beloved, a lover of the Omnipresent, a lover of mankind. His study of Torah makes him meek and reverent, and fits him to become just, pious, upright, and faithful; it also keeps him far from sin, and brings him close to virtue. Through him the world enjoys good counsel and sound knowledge. He is made like an everflowing fountain; he becomes modest, patient, and forgiving of insults, and it magnifies and exalts him above all things.

—*Rabbi Meir*

TRADITION

Tradition is a [protective] fence for the Torah. Tithes protect wealth, vows protect abstinence, silence protects wisdom.

—*Rabbi Akiva*

The Jewish tradition itself was one of reason and intellectual discipline, and besides that, a somewhat despised minority had a strong emotional interest to defeat the powers of darkness, of irrationality, of superstition, which blocked the road to its own emancipation and progress.

—*Erich Fromm*

TREE

If you have a sapling in your hand and someone says, "Behold, there is the messiah," go on with your planting and only then go out and welcome him.

—*Johanan ben Zakkai*

If a man kills a tree before its time, it is as though he murdered a soul.

—*Rabbi Nahman of Bratslav*

Trees were created for man's companionship.

—*Genesis Rabbah*

You must not destroy [a besieged city's] trees. You may eat of them, but you must not cut them down.

—*Deuteronomy*

TROUBLE

One does not meet trouble halfway.

—*Rava*

Little troubles are really a good thing—for someone else.

—*Shalom Aleichem*

The house is on fire, but the clock keeps ticking.

—*Yiddish saying*

The troubles of many are a half-solace.

—*Dutch Jewish saying*

A person doesn't live from happy occasions, and he doesn't die from troubles.

—*Yiddish saying*

TRUST

A fool is one who trusts another fool.

—*Sephardic saying*

Put your trust in the Lord.

—*Psalms*

Don't be quick to believe, and don't be surprised.

—*Yiddish saying*

TRUTH

There is no opposition between the truth of God and the salvation of Israel.

—*Martin Buber*

If you are proved right, you gain little, but if you are proved wrong you gain much—you learn the truth.

—*Judah ben Samuel*

A truth does not become greater through repetition.

—*Maimonides*

Sometimes, even liars tell the truth.

—*Moses ibn Ezra*

Truth bears a halo.

—*Samuel Hanagid*

Endure the truth, even if it be bitter.

—*Solomon ibn Gabirol*

TYRANNY

God does not deal tyrannically with His creatures.

—*Talmud*

It is better to grow wings and fly away, than submit to a godless king.

—*Esther Rabbah*

UNDERSTANDING

The longer a blind man lives, the more he sees.

—*Shalom Aleichem*

A sage understands two words from one.

—*Yiddish saying*

A wise man understands with a hint, a donkey needs a fist.

—*Moroccan Jewish saying*

It is impossible to understand the fundamentals of creation, how all segments are closely tied and wonderfully arranged, unless we infer the unity of the Creator and of reality.

—*Vilna Gaon*

UNITY

Everything above and below is one unity.

—*Baal Shem Tov*

Two are always stronger!

—*Yiddish saying*

USURY

Whoever does not lend money on interest, either to a Jew or Gentile, walks with honor.

—*Talmud*

The usurer has no fear of God. God says, "Whoever lives on usury in this world will not inhabit the next world."

—*Exodus Rabbah*

VALOR

Whoever does not take risks will not get profits.

—*Sephardic saying*

When the cat's not home, the mice jump on the table.

—*Dutch Jewish saying*

Who can find a woman of valor? Her price is far above rubies.

—*Proverbs*

VALUE

The more valuable an object, the more effort it demands.

—*Saadiah Gaon*

What value is a needle without an eye?

—*Yiddish saying*

The mountain gave birth to a mouse.

—*Iraqi Jewish saying*

VANITY

Nobody is as ugly as a self-satisfied man.

—*Hassidic saying*

A giant in your eyes may be a dwarf in ours.

—*Genesis Rabbah*

VICTORY

The race is not to the swift, nor the battle to the strong.

—*Ecclesiastes*

In defeat we are victorious, in death we are reborn.

—*Sholem Asch*

VIOLENCE

Violence breeds violent succession.
—*Solomon ibn Gabirol*

If the Bible, then no sword. If the sword, then no Bible.

—*Talmud*

VIRTUE

Envy a man nothing, except his virtue.
—*Eleazar ben Judah of Worms*

Virtue flowing from reason is superior to virtue not founded on reason.
—*Shneur Zalman*

In every age, virtue has been exceedingly spare.
—*Baruch Spinoza*

Why did God create only one man? So that virtue and vice will not be called hereditary.
—*Talmud*

VISITING

Whoever neglects to visit a sick person is like one who sheds blood.
—*Rabbi Akiva*

Visiting is like rain: prayed for when absent, and tiresome when overdone.

—*Talmud*

Let your foot be seldom in your neighbor's house.

—*Proverbs*

WAGES

Wages are payable at the conclusion of the work.

—*Talmud*

As you sow, so shall you reap.

—*Yemenite Jewish saying*

WALKING

If you don't walk four cubits after a meal, you won't digest your food.

—*Talmud*

WAR

War never ends war.

—*Stephen S. Wise*

Sweets are not handed out during a war.

—*Sephardic saying*

A bad peace is better than a good war.

—*Yiddish saying*

WEAKNESS

Few people are bad, but many are weak.

—*Louis D. Brandeis*

Separate reeds are weak and easily broken;
when tied together they are hard to tear apart.

—*Midrash*

WEALTH

Who is wealthy? The man with a virtuous wife.

—*Rabbi Akiva*

Some people are chained—to gold and silver.

—*Talmud*

When a man's wealth diminishes, even his children reject his opinion.

—*Solomon ibn Gabirol*

Whoever has a great deal, wants more.

—*Sephardic saying*

Why snatch at wealth, and hoard and stock it? Your shroud, you know, will have no pocket.

—*Betty Paoli*

WICKEDNESS

It is beyond man's power to explain the prosperity of the wicked or the troubles of the good.

—Ethics of the Fathers

Six things the Lord hates, seven are an abomination to Him: haughty eyes, a lying tongue, hands that shed innocent blood, a heart that devises wicked thought, feet that are swift in running to evil, a false witness that breathes out lies, and he that sows discord among brothers.

—Proverbs

WIFE

Give your ear to all, your hand to friends, but your lips only to your wife.

—Yiddish saying

A man without a wife is not a man.

—Talmud

Who finds a wife, finds great good.

—Proverbs

Find joy in the wife of your youth.

—*Proverbs*

WINE

Wine whets the appetite.

—*Talmud*

Old wine is good for the stomach.

—*Talmud*

Where there is no wine, drugs are necessary.

—*Talmud*

WISDOM/WISE

Great men are not always wise.

—*Job*

Wisdom is a tree whose fruit is virtue.

—*Rabbinical saying*

The beginning of wisdom is to desire it.
—*Solomon ibn Gabirol*

Better a slap from a wise man than a kiss from a fool.

—*Yiddish saying*

The words of the wise are heard in the quiet.
—*Ecclesiastes*

Who is wise? He who learns from all men.
—*Ethics of the Fathers*

Life is a dream for the wise, a game for the fool, a comedy for the rich, a tragedy for the poor.

—*Shalom Aleichem*

WOMAN

Every woman has a mind of her own.
—*Talmud*

It is a duty to save a woman from rape, even at the cost of the assailant's life.

—*Simeon bar Yochai*

Reading a poem in translation is like kissing a woman through a veil.

—*Chaim Nahman Bialik*

If the vision of a beautiful woman, or of any lovely thing, comes suddenly to mind, let a man say to himself: The source of such beauty must be from the divine source which permeates the universe. So why be attracted by a part? Better be drawn after the All. Perception of beauty is an experience of the Eternal.

—*Baal Shem Tov*

The Bible is the only literature in the world, up to our own century, which looks at women as human beings, no better and no worse than men.

—*Edith Hamilton*

WORDS

Judge your words before you utter them.
—*Talmud*

Pleasant words are like a honeycomb—sweet to the soul, and health to the bones.
—*Proverbs*

A kind word is no substitute for a piece of herring.
—*Shalom Aleichem*

The instruments of both life and death are contained within the power of the tongue.
—*Proverbs*

WORLD

If I love God, what need have I of the world to come?

—*Baal Shem Tov*

As a house implies a builder, a dress a weaver, a door a carpenter, so the world proclaims God, its Creator.

—*Rabbi Akiva*

God does not play dice with the world.
—*Albert Einstein*

When a man falls into his anecdotage, it is a sign for him to retire from the world.
—*Benjamin Disraeli*

We live in a divine world.
—*Samson Raphael Hirsch*

The world unites and reconciles all contradictions: all souls and spirits, all events and all things, all desires, drives and enthusiasms, everything is part of a large order and kingdom. God is King.

—*Rav Kook*

He who saves one soul, it is as though he saved the world.

—*Talmud*

WORRY

Worry over what has not occurred is a serious illness.

—*Solomon ibn Gabirol*

Everyone worries—some because their pearls are too sparse, others because the beans in their soup are too sparse.

—*Yiddish saying*

Worry saps a man's strength.

—*Talmud*

WORTH

If a husband and wife are worthy, the Divine Presence abides with them; if they are not, fire consumes them.

—*Rabbi Akiva*

YOUTH

Youth is a blunder, manhood a struggle, old age a regret.

—*Benjamin Disraeli*

Do not be deceived by the outward appearance of age or youth—a new pitcher may be full of good, old wine, while an old one may be totally empty.

—*Judah Hanassi*

To seek wisdom in old age is like a mark in the sand. To seek wisdom in youth is like engraving on stone.

—*Solomon ibn Gabirol*

If I don't acquire ideals when young, when will I? Not when I am old.

—*Maimonides*

ZION

The Lord dwells in Zion.

—*Joel*

SOURCES

NOTE: Certain terms and concepts should be explained, as they appear below. The abbreviations BCE and CE are comparable to B.C. and A.D.; they mean Before the Common Era, and Common Era.

Ashkenazic refers to central and eastern Europe; *Sephardic* refers to Spain, Portugal and the Mediterranean area.

There are sayings ascribed to a given Jewish community, such as "Persian Jewish saying." These have been handed down from generation to generation and are offered without an individual's attribution.

The word Rabbah after a biblical book refers

to the Midrash Rabbah, the classic homiletic commentaries on the Bible.

The word "Torah" is technically the first third of the Jewish Bible, i.e., the Pentateuch, also known as the Five Books of Moses. The term is also used to encompass all of the Bible, as well as all of the Jewish religion and belief.

The "Wisdom of Sirach," included in the Apocrypha, is also known as Ecclesiasticus.

"Proverbs" refers to the Book of Proverbs in the Bible.

Hassidic refers to the relatively new ultra-Orthodox movement within Judaism that stresses mystical adherence to Jewish law.

ABBA ARICHA Babylonian rabbi-scholar, affectionately known as "Abba the Tall."

ABBAYE Fourth-century rabbi who led famed Pumbedeita academy.

GRACE AGUILAR Nineteenth-century British author who wrote for women.

AHIKAR Aramaic book of wisdom literature. Only translations survive.

APOCRYPHA Jewish religion texts, written between 200 BCE and 200 CE, which were not included in Hebrew Bible.

RABBI AKIVA One of Judaism's greatest rabbis, who, it is believed, did not learn to read until mid-life.

HANNAH ARENDT Sociologist and scholar who wrote on Holocaust. Died in 1976.

SHOLEM ASCH Yiddish novelist and dramatist. Born in Poland in 1880, lived in U.S., died in Israel in 1957.

BAAL SHEM TOV Founder of Hassidic movement. Born in 1700, died in 1760. He was known as a healer and wonder worker.

LEO BAECK Leading German Reform rabbi and communal leader, who survived Nazi concentration camp. Died in London in 1956.

BARUCH One of the Apocrypha's volumes, believed to have been written after destruction of Jerusalem's Temple in 586 BCE.

BERNARD BARUCH Advisor to U.S. presidents, he was a financial wizard, and regarded as an elder statesman. Born in South Carolina, he died at age 95 in 1965.

SIMEON BAR YOCHAI Rabbinical authority and mystic; he lived in the second century CE. His mentor was Rabbi Akiva.

VICKI BAUM American author who wrote popular novels. Died in 1960.

SIMEON BEN ELIEZER Second-century scholar of Mishna (Oral Law), he lived in Tiberias. His mentor was Rabbi Meir.

DAVID BEN GURION First prime minister of Israel, generally regarded as the architect of the Jewish state. Died at age 86 in 1973.

ELEAZAR BEN JUDAH OF WORMS Mystic and religious scholar, he lived in medieval Germany in the 12th and 13th centuries.

SIMEON BEN LAKISH A gladiator in his teens, he became a leading third-century Talmudic scholar.

JUDAH BEN SAMUEL Lived in Regensburg in the 12th century; considered a supremely pious and humble person.

JOHANAN BEN ZAKKAI Major Jewish leader following the Romans' destruction of the Holy Temple in Jerusalem in 70 CE.

ITZHAK BEN ZVI Second president of Israel, he was a respected scholar of esoteric, dispersed Jewish communities.

HENRI BERGSON Nobel Laureate, French philosopher. Vichy France offered him exemption from Nazi racial laws; he declined, registered as a Jew, and died in 1941.

CHAIM NAHMAN BIALIK The father of modern Hebrew poetry. Born in a Ukrainian village in 1873, he died in Tel Aviv in 1934.

BOKHARAN JEWISH SAYING Bokhara, sometimes spelled Bukhara, was a center of Jewish population among Moslems for many centuries in what is today Turkestan and Uzbekistan.

LOUIS D. BRANDEIS The first Jewish justice to serve on the U.S. Supreme Court. In his earlier years he was known as the "people's attorney." Born in Louisville, Kentucky, in 1856, he died in 1941.

B'RURIAH Fourth-century Talmudic scholar; only woman taken seriously by fellow scholars of her time. Her husband was famed Rabbi Meir.

MARTIN BUBER Theologian and philosopher who stressed the need for religious dialogue. Born in Vienna in 1878, he died in Jerusalem in 1965.

MARC CHAGALL Internationally acclaimed artist whose works are on permanent display in the world's major museums.

CENTRAL EUROPEAN JEWISH SAYING Words of wisdom that are attributed to Jewish communities of Germany, Belgium, Holland, and Czechoslovakia.

CHOFETZ CHAIM Rabbinical scholar who stressed constant need to live by highest moral codes. He was born in Poland in 1838 and died there in 1933.

DEUTERONOMY The fifth book of the Five Books of Moses, or Torah.

BENJAMIN DISRAELI British statesman and author. Although he was baptized at 13, he took a lifelong pride in his Jewish origins.

DUTCH JEWISH SAYING Many early settlers in Holland, as of the 16th century, were refugees fleeing from the Inquisition in Spain.

ECCLESIASTES One of the most thought-provoking books of the Bible. Known in Hebrew as *Kohelet*.

ECCLESIASTES RABBAH Midrashic commentary on Ecclesiastes.

EGYPTIAN JEWISH SAYING Although the Jewish community in modern Egypt is minuscule today, Jews have lived in Egypt for millenia.

ALBERT EINSTEIN One of the twentieth century's greatest scientists. A Nobel Laureate in physics, he was invited to become president of Israel, an honor he declined with profound thanks.

ESTHER RABBAH Midrashic commentary on the biblical book Esther, which recounts the Purim story.

ETHICS OF THE FATHERS A section of the Talmud that contains pithy words of wisdom, chosen from the teachings of various rabbis and scholars. Traditionally this text is studied during the long, hot summers on Sabbath afternoons.

EXODUS RABBAH Midrashic commentary on the Hebrew Bible's second book.

EZEKIEL   One of the three major biblical prophets, the others being Isaiah and Jeremiah.

EDNA FERBER   Popular U.S. novelist and playwright. Born in 1887, she died in 1968.

EDMOND FLEG   A French writer who died in 1963, he developed a strong commitment to Judaism and Zionism following the notorious Dreyfus trial.

FRENCH JEWISH SAYING   Although Jews in France were massacred and expelled, and the Talmud was burned in Paris on orders of the church, Jews continued to live there for many centuries.

SIGMUND FREUD   Founder of psychoanalysis. Born in Moravia in 1856, he grew up in Vienna, fled the Nazis in 1938, and died in London the next year.

ERICH FROMM   Descended from a rabbinical family, he was a prominent social psychologist, who called himself an atheist. Late in life, he took a renewed interest in Judaism. He died in 1980, at age 80.

GENESIS   The first book of the Hebrew Bible.

GENESIS RABBAH   Midrashic commentary on Genesis.

GERMAN JEWISH SAYING Attributed to scattered Jewish communities in what eventually came to be a united German state.

HENRY GEORGE A 19th-century American economist who promoted the single tax concept. He was not Jewish.

HABAKUK One of the minor prophets in the Bible, he lived in the seventh century BCE.

HAI GAON In the 10th and 11th centuries, he headed the Babylonian academy. He was the top religious leader of the East.

JUDAH HALEVI One of the greatest Spanish-Jewish poets and philosophers. He lived in the 11th and 12th centuries.

EDITH HAMILTON Author and educator. Born in 1867, she died in 1963. She was not Jewish.

HASSIDIC SAYING Although there are conflicting groups within the Hassidic movement, some sayings are common to all.

HEINRICH HEINE One of Germany's greatest poets and philosophers of the 19th century, he was baptized at 28, an act he later regretted.

WILL HERBERG U.S. author, educator and philosopher, best known for his book, *Judaism and Modern Man,* published in 1951.

THEODOR HERZL Founder of the world Zionist movement, he was a playwright and journalist. He predicted in 1897 that in 50 years a Jewish state would arise—Israel was proclaimed in 1948. He died at the age of 44.

ABRAHAM JOSHUA HESCHEL One of the greatest Jewish theologians and rabbis of the 20th century, who taught hundreds of rabbinical students. He died in 1972.

HILLEL A leading sage of the Second Temple Era, he was known for his gentle, lenient interpretations of Jewish law.

SAMSON RAPHAEL HIRSCH A 19th-century religious thinker and rabbi, he developed a unique style of Orthodox Jewish observance.

HOSEA One of the minor prophets, who lived in the eighth century BCE.

HUNGARIAN JEWISH SAYING Jews in Hungary were sharply divided between extremely Orthodox and assimilationist groups.

SOL HUROK Noted American impresario, who died in 1974.

ABRAHAM IBN EZRA Bible commentator, grammarian, poet, and scientist. He was born in Spain in 1092, and died there in 1167.

MOSES IBN EZRA Leading Spanish-Jewish poet of the 11th century, who produced over 500 religious and secular poems.

SOLOMON IBN GABIROL Tragic poet and philosopher of 11th-century Spain, he died at age 37. Many of his poems are in the Jewish liturgy.

BAHYA IBN PAKUDA Religious judge and philosopher of 11th-century Spain. He wrote *Duties of the Heart*, an ethics work.

JUDAH IBN TIBBON Translator who lived in 12th-century France, he worked with Arabic texts that he produced in Hebrew.

IRAQI JEWISH SAYING Although Iraq today is virtually without a Jewish community, the ancient Babylonian community there was more than two millenia old.

ISAIAH One of the Bible's three major prophets, the other two being Jeremiah and Ezekiel.

ISRAELI JEWISH SAYING Although Israel is still a very young country, it is steadily growing an impressive culture of its own, some of it rooted in ancient Judea, and some influenced by 2,000 years of exile.

ITALIAN JEWISH SAYING Jews have lived continuously in Italy since they were brought to ancient Rome as slaves of their conquerors in the year 70 CE.

JEREMIAH One of the major prophets, the other two being Ezekiel and Isaiah.

JOB One of the most difficult and poignant biblical books.

JOEL One of the 13 minor prophets.

JOSHUA The book of Joshua recounts the story of Moses's successor and his capture of the Land of Israel for the former Hebrew slaves, who completed their 40 years of wandering through the wilderness.

JUDAH HANASSI Credited with compiling the Mishna, the basic text of oral Jewish law. Led Israel's Jews in the difficult 2nd and 3rd centuries CE.

JUDITH One of the books included in the Apocrypha.

FRANZ KAFKA Born in 1883, he was a writer whose poor health led to an early death in 1924. In his final years he voiced a renewed interest in Judaism.

MORDECAI KAPLAN Born in Vilna (now Vilnius) in 1881, he died in New York in 1983. Founder of the Reconstructionist wing of Judaism, he was an American-Jewish religious innovator and theologian.

KURDISTAN JEWISH SAYING Virtually the entire, ancient Jewish community from this central Asian area has moved to Israel.

RABBI LEVI ISAAC OF BERDICHEV Noted Hassidic rabbi of 18th century, he began as a rabbinical scholar, but later espoused the Hassidic view.

LEVITICUS Third book of the Bible.

LEVITICUS RABBAH Midrashic commentary on Leviticus.

MOSES LUZZATTO 18th-century, Italian-born scholar, mystic, and poet. He purportedly thought of himself as a messianic harbinger, and was in frequent conflict with rabbinical leaders.

SAMUEL LUZZATTO Italian rabbi and Bible scholar of the 19th century who opposed Jewish mysticism, stressing need for traditional observance.

EDGAR MAGNIN American Reform rabbi and communal leader in California.

MALACHI One of the minor prophets.

MAIMONIDES The greatest Jewish personality since biblical days. He was a rabbi, physician, philosopher, and communal leader, and his ideas continue to influence Jewry to this day. Also known as Rambam.

GOLDA MEIR The most outstanding Jewish woman of the 20th century. She served as Israel's prime minister and died in 1978.

RABBI MEIR Known as an "architect of the Mishna" in the second century, he was married to B'ruriah, the leading woman religious scholar.

MEKILTA (EXODUS) A Midrashic commentary on the latter section of Exodus, the Bible's second book.

MENDELE MOCHER SEFORIM Acclaimed as the "grandfather of Yiddish literature," he wrote in both Yiddish and Hebrew. He died in 1917.

MOSES MENDELSSOHN Scholar, philosopher, and communal leader, he was the outstanding personality of Germany's Jews in the 18th century.

MICAH One of the minor prophets, who lived at the time of Isaiah.

MIDRASH Literature of scriptural interpretation designed to elicit moral lessons or religious-legal points from the biblical text.

CLAUDE MONTEFIORE British scholar and educator. He died in 1938.

MOROCCAN JEWISH SAYING Although the overwhelming majority of Morocco's Jews have moved to Israel, there is still a sizable Jewish community in that country.

RABBI NAHMAN OF BRATSLAV Born in 1772, he was a charismatic Hassidic rabbi and founder of the Bratslav sect. He was a great-grandson of the Baal Shem Tov, founder of Hassidism. Rabbi Nahman died in 1811.

NAHMANIDES A leading Bible commentator, scholar, and communal leader, he was also a physician. He was born in Spain in 1194, where he died in 1270.

MAX NORDAU An early psychiatrist, he was one of the first Zionist leaders who worked closely with Theodor Herzl. He died in 1923.

NUMBERS The fourth book of the Bible.

NUMBERS RABBAH Midrashic commentary on Numbers.

BETTY PAOLI A 19th-century German-Jewish poet.

PERSIAN JEWISH SAYING The Iranian (Persian) Jewish community is very ancient. Jews in Iran today are believed to number over 20,000, and are regarded as virtual hostages.

PHILO Jewish religious thinker, influenced by Greek philosophy which he sought to blend with Jewish teachings. Born 25 BCE, died 50 CE.

PROVERBS Book of Proverbs, one of the Bible's most beautiful sections.

PSALMS A mainstay of the Bible, recited often during times of need.

RABBINICAL SAYING Traditional comment, passed down through the generations, with no accurate attribution possible.

RASHI Born in Troyes, France, in 1040, this outstanding scholar died in 1105. He is universally regarded as the greatest Jewish commentator and interpreter of the Bible and Talmud.

RAV KOOK First chief rabbi of modern Palestine's Jewish community, he was admired by religious and secular Jews. He died in 1935.

RAVA Babylonian rabbi who lived in the fourth century CE, and founded a major religious school.

THEODORE REIK A psychoanalyst and student of Freud, he fled the Nazis in the 1930s and settled in the U.S. He died in 1969.

NAHIDA REMY A German-Jewish author, she was born in 1849 and died in 1927.

FRANZ ROSENZWEIG A German-Jewish philosopher and educator who at one time almost let himself be talked into converting to Christianity. Instead he became an observant Jew, and left a treasure of religious writings.

CECIL ROTH An outstanding Jewish historian

and scholar, he was the author of numerous historical books.

SAADIAH GAON The greatest scholar of Babylonian Jewry. He was born in 882, died in 942. Credited with formulating the Jewish calendar still in worldwide use. Was also active as communal leader.

ISRAEL SALANTER Rabbi and founder of *musar* (morality) movement in Judaism. A rabbi, he stressed ethical-religious living. Died in 1883.

JESSIE SAMPTER An early woman Zionist leader and an admired poet. Born in 1883, she died in 1938.

SAMUEL I A prophet and judge, he lived in the 11th century BCE, and helped Israelites create a monarchy-type government.

SAMUEL HANAGID Statesman, scholar, poet, and communal leader in Moslem Spain in the 11th century.

HERBERT SAMUEL British statesman, member of a distinguished British Jewish family. He was first high commissioner of Palestine during the British mandatory period.

MAURICE SAMUEL Distinguished American-

Jewish author, translator, and lecturer. He helped popularize Shalom Aleichem. Died in 1972.

SOLOMON SCHECHTER Rabbinical scholar, who discovered 100,000 invaluable Jewish manuscripts and remnants in Cairo synagogues at the turn of the century. Served as president of Jewish Theological Seminary in New York.

ARTHUR SCHNITZLER Dramatist and scientific researcher, he was also a physician, who wrote prolifically. Born in Vienna, he died in 1931.

SEPHARDIC SAYING The Sephardic Jews originated in the Iberian peninsula as well as the Mediterranean basin area.

SHALOM ALEICHEM Often called the "Jewish Mark Twain," he was the foremost Jewish humorist. When he died in New York in 1931, hundreds of thousands of people turned out for the funeral procession.

BARUCH SPINOZA Born in Amsterdam, he was the son of Portuguese Jews who fled the Inquisition. Rabbinical authorities disapproved of his secular studies, including Latin and philosophy, and excommunicated him in 1656 for heresy. Efforts are under way to rescind the excommunication. He died in 1677.

TALMUD The two major commentaries—Mishna and Gemara—together form the Talmud. Essentially this contains eight centuries of learned study and disputations on various points of Jewish law, offered by generations of great scholars.

TOBIT One of the books included in the Apocrypha.

LEO TOLSTOY One of the world's leading novelists, he was also a liberal religious philosopher in his native Russia. He was not Jewish; he died in 1910.

TOSEFTA (KIDDUSHIN) An additional commentary on a talmudic tractate; Kiddushin deals with marriage.

TUNISIAN JEWISH SAYING Almost all Tunisian Jews moved to Israel.

MARK TWAIN Probably America's best-known humorist; he was born in 1835 and died in 1910. He was not Jewish.

RACHEL VARNHAGEN An influential German-Jewish literary patron, best-known as a salon hostess. She inspired Heine, backed Goethe, and was admired in virtually all cultural circles. She died in 1833.

VILNA GAON Born in 1720, he was a world-respected rabbinical authority who greatly influenced east European Jewry. He strongly opposed mystical Hassidism, stressing need for rational understanding of Torah. He died in 1797.

BARBARA WARD Noted economist and author both in the United States and England, she was born in 1914 and died in 1981. She was not Jewish.

GEORGE WASHINGTON First president of the United States. He was not Jewish.

CHAIM WEIZMANN First president of Israel, he devoted his whole life to realization of the Zionist dream. He was a renowned chemist.

FRANZ WERFEL Born in 1890, this sensitive author, poet, and translator was baptized after his death, at the request of his wife, who had been the widow of Gustav Mahler. He died in 1945.

WISDOM OF SIRACH A volume in the Apocrypha, it is also known as Ecclesiasticus.

STEPHEN S. WISE A leading American rabbi and political activist, he was a confidant of President Franklin Roosevelt. He died in 1949.

HARRY WOLFSON A long-time professor of the history of philosophy and Hebrew literature at Harvard. He was born in 1874, received an intensive religious education, and died in 1974.

YIDDISH SAYING Yiddish was the lingua franca of the Jews of Russia, Poland, the Baltics, Romania, and, to a lesser extent, several other countries.

YEMENITE JEWISH SAYING The isolated Jews of Yemen were brought to Israel in a dramatic air rescue. A small number still remain in Yemen.

SHNEUR ZALMAN Founder of the Habad sect of Hassidism, he promoted more study and scholarship among his followers. The Lubavich Hassidic sect today adheres to his teachings. He died in 1813.

ISRAEL ZANGWILL Prolific British-Jewish author and satirist. Sought to set up a Jewish homeland in any secure part of the world, coming into conflict with Zionist movement. He died in 1926.

ZOHAR The primary work of Jewish mysticism.

STEFAN ZWEIG Poet, dramatist, and biographer. Fled Nazis, lived in England, U.S., and Brazil. Committed suicide in 1942.

ACKNOWLEDGMENTS

We have consulted many, many volumes—in English, Hebrew, and Yiddish—in our search for the most relevant and apt proverbs and wise sayings for this book. A special thanks should be noted for the excellent sources and material found in these books:

Babylonian Talmud, Soncino Press, London (1952).

Holy Scriptures (Masoretic text), Jewish Publication Society, Philadelphia (1917).

Tanakh, A New Translation of Holy Scriptures, Jewish Publication Society, Philadelphia (1985).

Authorized Daily Prayer Book, Joseph Hertz. Bloch Publishing Co., New York (1948).

Apocrypha, translated by Edgar J. Goodspeed, University of Chicago Press, Chicago (1938).

A Treasury of Jewish Quotations, Joseph L. Baron. Crown Publishers, New York (1956).

Treasury of Jewish Quotations, Leo Rosten. McGraw-Hill, New York (1972).

Dictionary of Jewish Biography, Geoffrey Wigoder. Simon & Schuster, New York (1991).

Proverbs of Eastern Communities (Hebrew), Abraham Shtal. Am Oved, Tel Aviv (1978).

INDEX OF TOPICS

"If you want to give God a good laugh,
tell him your plans."
—Yiddish Folk Saying

*If you want more pearls of wisdom from
great Jewish personalities and thinkers,
head to your nearest bookstore.*

GREAT JEWISH QUOTES:
Five Thousand Years of Truth and Humor
From the Bible to George Burns

by Noah benShea

A quality trade paperback now available in bookstores.
Published by Ballantine Books.